MAJESTIC

IS

YOUR

NAME

Rekindling the Inner Fire Devotional Series

REKINDLING
THE INNER FIRE

◆ ◆ ◆ ◆ ◆ ◆ ◆ ◆ ◆ ◆ ◆

MAJESTIC IS YOUR NAME

◆

*A 40-Day Journey
in the Company of*

THERESA OF AVILA

*Devotional Readings Arranged
and Paraphrased by*

David Hazard

◆

BETHANY HOUSE PUBLISHERS
MINNEAPOLIS, MINNESOTA 55438

Published by Bethany House Publishers
A Ministry of Bethany Fellowship, Inc.
6820 Auto Club Road, Minneapolis, Minnesota 55438

Printed in the United States of America

Library of Congress Cataloging-in-Publication Data

Theresa of Avila, Saint, 1515-1582.
   [Selections. English. 1993]
   Majestic is your name : a 40-day journey in the company of Theresa of Avila : devotional readings / arranged by David Hazard.
      p. cm. — (Rekindling the inner fire)
   Translated from the Spanish.
   1. Spiritual life—Catholic Church—Early works to 1800. 2. Meditations—Early works to 1800. I. Hazard, David. II. Title. III. Series.
BX2179.T3E5   1993
242—dc20   93–8114
ISBN 1–55661–336–9   CIP

To MaryLynne
who has patiently trusted the Lord
for me.

Foreword

O Lord, our Lord, how majestic is your name in all the earth!

———

Psalm 8:1

She was known in her lifetime as Theresa of Jesus. When she spoke to her followers, and in her writings, she referred to her Lord as "His Majesty." So intense was her devotion that sixteenth-century Spain—which would first try to crush her, then try to claim ownership of her—was shaken to its foundations.

The young woman from the Castilian provincial town of Avila wanted only to imitate Jesus Christ. So deep was her desire to walk the path of her Lord's humility that she could not be provoked to speak a word in her own defense—not even when the Inquisition ordered that both Theresa and her writings be seized "for examination."

A whole drama presents itself, doesn't it? We see a lone young woman trying to live a pure

7

faith—and we watch her come under vicious attack by the very institution she loves. She submits herself, body and soul, to their intense pressure and scrutiny and, despite all that, she spearheads a vast spiritual revival. If Theresa were alive today, agents would be offering her film contracts.

Be careful not to form smug judgments about Theresa's spiritual superiors, though, or about the Catholic church of her day. If you have come to this devotional book hoping to get any benefit from Theresa's wisdom, you will find that her words radiate light deep inside and unsettle the dark dust that can blanket your innermost soul. And then you are forced to decide—not so much about her, as the Church was obligated to do— but what you must do about *yourself*.

Theresa's only desire was to let the Lord Jesus Christ live in her being, to see Him honored and praised through her life. How deadly dangerous this is for the half-Christian/half-worldling who is only toying with the faith.

So then, before you set out on this forty-day journey in the "company" of Theresa of Avila, you should know something about her life, and her spiritual fire—in the event that some sparks begin to ignite within you.

Theresa was born in March 1515, in a town in southern Spain. Avila was surrounded by thick walls, built a century before to withstand the Moors when they threatened to conquer Europe for Islam. The knights who once swaggered the streets had long been at rest in the church's graveyard. Gone were other vestiges of the heraldic and Christian past, as well.

Three centuries had passed since the last great spiritual light had blazed from the Italian hill town of Assisi. The Church was entering into a time of rapid secularization. Kepler identified new laws of gravity. Vesalius performed autopsies and laid groundwork for modern medicine. Copernicus advanced his observations about the solar system, which seemed to challenge the Church's statements about the earth and Man. Science and rational thinking was replacing otherworldly hopes and longings.

And, too, it was the age when nations were expanding their earthly horizons. Columbus had found his way to North America. Magellan planted his flag in the Philippines. Conquistadors were at war from Mexico to South America, and eastward in India. The Church could preach itself blue in the face about the terrors of hell and the treasures of heaven. For Europe's kings and queens, there were new lands to be claimed and colonized . . . and gold. For the merchant class, there were silks and spices to trade . . . and gold.

True, the Church wanted to shake off the superstition of the Middle Ages. But it was having a difficult time finding its authoritative voice: Science challenged its dogma, and an opening new world lured the faithful.

As if that were not enough. . . . In the year of Theresa's birth, Martin Luther trudged up the portal of a German cathedral and tacked up a list of ninety-five theses. What began as an attempt to reform doctrine rapidly heated into a struggle on the issue of authority. Before long, Calvin had established a second "Rome" in Geneva, Henry VIII had set up his own church, and John Knox had swayed Mary Queen of Scots over to his persuasions. The Council of Trent would wade through the litter, attempting to rescue the sovereign unity of the Church Universal. It was too late.

All told, the Church did not need any supernatural visionaries at this moment—let alone a *woman* whose vision would challenge the Church itself.

In one way, these upheavals were light-years distant from the home of the nobleman Don Alonso Sanchez de Cepeda, Theresa's father. His heart was founded on traditions of faith and honor. Just as his father had done, Don Alonso read to his family every evening from the lives of the saints or Christian heroes who had given their blood to defend the Cross.

So Theresa grew up playing "monks and nuns" with her little friends, and once convinced her brother to run away with her to find an Islamic hoard in the naive hope of being martyred for Christ. She vowed her life to God.

Theresa's mother had different tastes. She was

often ill, and often lay in bed devouring a series of popular novels about a "darkly handsome" knight, "Amadis of Gaul." It was medieval soap opera, which Don Alonso detested. When he was absent, she entertained her children by retelling the adventures of the romantic hero.

This minor deception had a bad influence on Theresa as she entered adolescence. She grew into a pretty young woman, who loved the flash of new silk, the glint of jewelry, parties, and the flattery of young men. Soon she was wrapped in worldly vanities, living in her own romantic dramas.

When a spiritual power seized the young woman of twenty—swiftly, strangely—she was little more than a shell of prettiness. Church and prayer were sheer drudgery, and her childhood vow was long forgotten. But somewhere within, a spark of longing for God burned. Reams have been written in speculation about the "illness" that felled Theresa like an arrow. In one stroke, she was trapped in weakening flesh for the rest of her life. Freud called it typical female hysteria. Some say epilepsy or narcolepsy. Anything but what it was: a wake-up call from eternity.

This is where Theresa's faith first slaps us on the cheek. We resist the view that an older spiritual wisdom offers, because sickness saps our strength and drive, and tears away the road map we try to draw for our lives.

On a clear-blue Castilian day, Theresa

dropped unexpectedly, like a dead woman. No pulse. Skin growing cold. Physicians found no trace of life. Nuns at the local convent laid out the stiffening body for burial, where it remained for several days.

What a shock when, like Jairus' daughter called back to life by Jesus, Theresa's eyes fluttered, limbs moved, and color bled into her cheeks. She was alive, but in great pain.

All was changed. What gentleman wanted to court a stunning woman who might collapse like a corpse in mid-kiss? Again and again, Theresa fell without warning into her strange, living deaths.

In a short time, Theresa joined Avila's Convent of the Incarnation. The women there were called "Carmelites," because they had inherited the practices of prayer that came down to them from early Christians who had built lonely places for retreat on Palestine's Mt. Carmel. Theresa's obsession with the world was over.

How disappointing to find that the world had invaded her retreat. The people of Avila trooped in daily, and they saved their most delicious cakes, meats, and gossip for the holy women of the Incarnation. Theresa was appalled, wanting only to retreat from such vanities because they captivated her so much. She had no idea that this simple wish would bring her a lifetime of trouble and harassment.

For now, she had other worries. The strange spells continued. For days, even weeks, she fell dead. Every waking moment was filled with pain. For years, she felt bored with prayer, lukewarm toward God, and unworthy to be a follower of Christ.

Then, it would seem, He came.

Theresa agonized all her life, and found it impossible with human language to explain the "appearances" of Jesus. She "saw" Him with the eyes of her heart. She caught sight of a new type of beauty that came from of old and extended to everlasting—and a holiness that walked among sinful men, lofty in its intense humility.

The taste of heaven was so sweet that Theresa understood in a moment how a worldly spirit clung to her, despite the outward appearance that she had forsaken all for God. She had given up exactly nothing in comparison with the new offer to know Christ in His humility and complete obedience. Living apart from normal humans was not enough. Wearing simpler clothes and saying more prayers was not enough, either. Forget all outward signs—this was a clear call to live a life separated to God *in heart*.

Once again Theresa's life witnessed challenges: How much of the world do we allow to invade our souls? How many "offerings" do we wave at God—our church attendance, our Bible reading—when we are really telling Him, "Only this far, God. No further, please"? How often do we want heavenly salvation *and* the world?

Imagine her superiors' reaction when, in confidence, she explained that Jesus Christ "appeared" to her invisibly, and "spoke" to her without words, in the front parlor. Spain had just been embarrassed by a woman from Cordoba who had fooled the Queen and the Grand Inquisitor before admitting her visions were made up . . . for which she was burned. The Reformation was in full force, ripping apart the Church. Who needed the additional hassle, if this was another crazy heretic?

Theresa was about thirty when she asked her superiors to let her start a home for Christian women who wanted to live a life more completely separated to God—in prayer, service to the poor, and meager living. She had no idea this would insult her superiors in the Church. Immediately, followers were drawn to her, including men like Brother John, of the Carmelites, who would become known as John of the Cross. They came, not because Theresa claimed to see Christ, which rumor spread, but because her life imitated His. When she spoke about "His Majesty," they sensed His presence.

Theresa's simple request touched off a madness of jealousy, controversy, and turmoil. This is important: She never used her supernatural "visions" to press her requests—she only wanted freedom to imitate Christ more.

For the remaining decades of her life, Theresa was alternately granted permission to plant her vision—then opposed and accused. Church leaders tried to crush her, and princes knelt before her in repentance. She was thrown in prison, her writings seized, her followers beaten, and she narrowly escaped the Inquisitor's rack and the stake. Eventually, she would found homes throughout Spain.

Against her own wishes, and despite pain and fatigue, Theresa always obeyed her superiors' orders and wrote about her life and beliefs—always knowing that her words would be sifted and her soul dissected by enemies. She wrote her spiritual biography, *The Life of Theresa of Jesus*, *The Way of Perfection*, and *The Interior Castle*.

She accepted even the resistance against her as one more way in which God was working into her the character of Jesus Christ in His many sufferings. Why should a servant think she was better than her Master?

Near the very end of her life, we find her trudging in ankle-deep mud in a cold spring downpour. She was old and literally in heart failure, but did not balk for a minute: She was on a mission to set up yet another home for prayer and retreat. A shallow but rushing river broke the resolve of the small band that was with her. Theresa marched into the icy waters. And was swept downstream. While her followers screamed from the shore and the numbing waters battled her ailing body, Theresa was tempted to chastise the Lord for allowing so very much opposition.

Above the flood, she saw Him and heard His words: "This is how I treat the ones who want to be my close friends."

She knew what He meant: Friends of God depend on Him utterly, no matter the opposition or setback, and He shows His power and majesty in their weakness.

Still, she could not resist a wry bit of humor. "Ah, my Lord," she replied, "then it's no wonder you have so few."

Moments later, her rain-soaked and weeping followers heard someone laughing at them from the far bank. There stood their "mother" in the faith, wet and matted as a muskrat, but teasing them for their cowardice.

Again, we could give in to the temptation to freeze-frame on that picture of Theresa—as a heroic woman, standing under the pressures of a male-dominated Church hierarchy to be a living example of Christian faith and obedience. But we would miss the whole point.

The spiritual path that Theresa walked is laid out in the devotional entries that follow: *God calls us to come to Him, and if we want to walk in His fellowship, we must stop seeking our worth, comfort, and security in everything else.*

In preparing this volume—the fifth in this series—I'm indebted to the research, translations, and compilations of several people, most especially E. Allison Peers, (*The Way of Perfection*); Clayton Berg Jr., (*A Life of Prayer*); Kernan Kavanaugh, and Otilio Rodriguez, (*The Interior Castle*). It is arranged to welcome you into God's gracious presence so the Holy Spirit may gently search your heart and bring you into greater spiritual freedom in Christ.

Anyone who tries to walk the spiritual path in Christ already knows how painfully often you stub your foot on the worldly trinkets and comforts that clutter the soul's living room floor. May you seek Him, no matter what the world offers. May you stand for His Truth, no matter what others say. May you find that His name is majestic, in all your earthly dealings and in your soul.

My prayer is that the words of this book, combined with the eternal Word of God, will give you more light to see your way . . . and renew the spiritual fire within you.

David Hazard

Contents

MAJESTIC
IS
YOUR
NAME

1
My Heart, Your Throne

I was, in spirit, there in heaven and saw—oh, the glory of it!—a throne and someone sitting on it! Great bursts of light flashed forth from him as from a glittering diamond, or from a shining ruby, and a rainbow glowing like an emerald encircled his throne . . . the Eternal Living One!

"O Lord, you are worthy to receive the glory and the honor and the power, for you have created all things. . . ."

Revelation 4:2–3, 9, 11, TLB

Jesus said . . . "I go [to] prepare a place for you, [and] I will come back and take you to be with me that you also may be where I am."

John 14:3

*T*oday, I was praying and asking God to show me how to explain this life of the spirit to you, since I am under orders from my superior to do so. I want you to know the best and surest way to have a strong inner life with God, but I could not think where to begin. Then, as I was in intercession—in spirit, bowed before the throne of God on your behalf—the idea came.

You must begin by seeing that each of our souls is like a splendid castle. The castle is fashioned entirely out of the clearest crystal—better still, out of diamond. Because of this, you and everyone around you may look within to the very center, to the throne room itself, to the seat of majesty where one sovereign authority reigns over all that you do. And because the castle is perfectly clear, whatever authority it is that governs from this center of your soul will also be seen by all.

In this castle, there are many other rooms in which you may spend your time, just as in heaven there are many dwelling places, as Jesus told us (John 14:2). If you reflect on this very carefully, you will realize how apt a picture this is, because His Majesty, our Lord Jesus, told us that His kingdom is a spiritual one (John 18:36). And so the soul that is built on the spiritual foundation of His righteousness can be a heavenly paradise. In the soul that is awakened to this understanding—the soul that gives total reign to its Majesty—God takes His delight (Proverbs 8:31).

Now we know that God is a king so mighty,

so holy and wise, so rich in goodness—what do you think a castle will be like if He takes His delight in it? Would He create for himself a dark and miserable place? Surely not. Nothing can compare to the beauty and greatness of the soul in which our King dwells in His full majesty. No earthly fire can compare with the light of its blazing love. No bastions can compare with its ability to endure forever.

All this is a mystery that even the greatest intellect can never take in, just as no one can fully comprehend God. We may accept that it is true, though, because God himself tells us that He created us in His image and in His own likeness (Genesis 1:26).

So I will tell you from the outset, you will only exhaust yourself if you struggle to understand with human intellect this interior castle and its beauty. You must enter the castle with your *soul*.

And all the while, hold these truths in mind: While He is within us, He is still, also, the high and holy Creator and we are His creations. And there is a vast difference between our comprehension and His. He is Spirit, and we are flesh. How can we ever create with our own hands, by our poor efforts, a place fitting for His Majesty, since we cannot form the slightest conception of Him on our own?

We begin in this way: We choose to bring *all* things—our rebelling thoughts, will and emotions, and every external circumstance, however pleasant or miserable—and lay them at His feet.

In short, we start by allowing our sovereign King to govern—and in this way we begin to see, as through a mist, the first dim outlines of the castle He longs to reveal within us—an interior dwelling place of sublime dignity and great beauty.

THE INTERIOR CASTLE

My Majestic Father, you are love and righteousness. I know there is no dwelling place for me as beautiful, no place as eternal as in you.

Help me, today, as I begin to release the government of my inmost being and all my earthly circumstances to your wise and loving rule.

Teach me the wonders of your majestic name.

2
Offer of Life

Jesus said, "Make a tree good and its fruit will be good. . . . The good man brings good things out of the good stored up in him. . . ."

Matthew 12:33, 35

On each side of the river [flowing from the throne of God] stood the tree of life . . . yielding its fruit . . . and the leaves of the tree are for . . . healing. . . .

Revelation 22:2

If a spring is pure and clear, then all the streams that flow from it must also be clear. This is how the soul becomes when it understands how to live within God's grace.

The soul must first understand that God means for it to be planted like a tree in Him (Psalm 1:3)—that is, we may draw joy from the fact that nothing but life eternal and perfect goodness flow from God (1 John 5:20; 2:29). And when we allow these streams to flow through us,

27

we become pleasing in the eyes of both God and man.

But if we do not stay rooted in Him, how can there be any refreshment for us? How can there be any good fruit for others to enjoy? (John 15:1–17). Make no mistake, it is the *spring* that keeps the soul from withering and helps it produce good fruit.

Let me tell you what happens when a soul does not stay rooted in God's free offering of life and righteousness, or when it uproots itself by willful, deliberate sin. Because the soul always seeks another source of sustenance, it will quickly root itself next to a pool of stagnant, foul water. Then all the actions that flow from this soul will also be foul and stinking—they will give no life, and will bear no good fruit.

It is true that the soul which has once rooted itself in Christ can never lose all the brightness of its King. And now I will return to the first image of the soul—that of a clear diamond castle. Once the splendid Sun of Righteousness has come into the central throne room, the castle can never lose its bright glory.

And yet, by our foolish neglect, and by our willful sins, we can drape the whole castle with a black pall. And then we may as well be dead, for in practical fact we have blotted out the life that is offered to us from within. Understand—there is no affect on the radiant Sun, no affect on the castle. But the light and life within it is no use to anyone.

Oh, souls who were purchased by the blood of our King, Jesus Christ!—look at yourselves, take pity upon yourselves! How can it be that you know these spiritual truths, and yet you do not engage your own will to assist the King in removing the black pall that hangs like grave clothes over your interior castle, so that everyone may peer within its beautiful crystal walls and see the radiance of our King within? . . .

Lord Jesus, what utter misery it is to look at a soul that is separated by ignorance from this light—one who is deprived of your Light, which you freely offer to place within us if we will but give up turning back to the darkness! How miserable are all the rooms within such a soul— most especially because they were created by you to be warm and beautiful and welcoming.

And how disordered are the physical senses of such a person. Because true sight only comes to us when we first gain our spiritual sight, one who lives in spiritual blindness will always stumble and fall over circumstances and poor choices, which a spiritual man or woman could plainly see and avoid. Since they are blind, though, they can only govern their lives by their own poor wits, rather than by walking in the light of God's wisdom—living for what they can see and feel and hear and want. This is bad government, indeed. For then you are living only

29

in the realm of the prince of this world, who is Satan.

In short, when our lives are planted where the Devil reigns, what kind of life will that be? What kind of fruit do you suppose we will bear? . . .

May God in His mercy open the inward eyes of our souls, and deliver us from so great an evil. . . . We in ourselves, separated from God and living apart from His life and light, are vanity itself. We, and all that we do, will be nothing but a vapor. And when a wind blows, we will be gone.

THE INTERIOR CASTLE

My Ever-Living Father, open my eyes to your holiness, which flows into me in order to bring new life—which you offer freely.

3
Entering In

Surely . . . the upright shall dwell in thy presence.

Psalm 140:13, KJV

Whither shall I go from thy spirit? or whither shall I flee from thy presence? . . . lead me in the way everlasting.

Psalm 139:7, 24, KJV

Jesus replied, "Walk in [the Light] while you can. . . . Make use of the Light while there is still time; then you will become light bearers."

John 12:35–36, TLB

Consider again the splendid castle of your soul.

Now that you can picture such a thing in your mind, there is a very great danger for you. For it is never enough to know about spiritual things with your mind. Mental knowledge is not the

31

same thing as truly understanding from the center of your being, which results from experiencing and doing.

It is important that we examine how we are to get into the castle of the soul.

Immediately, some of you will think, "How ridiculous: If this *splendid castle* she is talking about is my soul—then I am already *in* it. Am I not my very soul? This is as ridiculous as telling me to go into a room I am already standing in."

Do not be so hasty to turn away.

In any house, there is a tremendous difference between one room and another. And many Christian souls are satisfied—for a time, at least—to stop and dwell just inside their own soul's castle, in a plain room near the outer walls, right next to the guards' chamber. They pray long lists of prayers, and they even pore over the Scriptures, thinking this is all there is to the Christian life. And when they stagnate in their inner growth, they are frustrated and confused.

The truth is, some are afraid to learn what lies deeper within that splendid castle—for they know He is a Sovereign power and, if once they catch sight of Him, He will command their full allegiance. And then their own will—their very self—must be changed to become one with His. As a result, they haven't the slightest idea that other rooms lie within them, nor the least idea what they are.

No wonder it sounds ridiculous, then, when a spiritual adviser tells them, "A soul must enter into itself," which many of the old devotional writers tell us. This is exactly what I am telling you to do.

A very wise man once said to me that a Christian who does not know about this deeper exercise of prayer is like one who lives in a crippled body, or like a paralytic. Although he has arms and legs he cannot use them, and so he puts up a struggle—only to be defeated again and again.

In the same way, there are souls so caught up in trying to conquer the turmoil of *external circumstances*, striving and striving to win over the world—even by their many prayers and spiritual works! Instead, they become weak in spirit, without the slightest idea of how to become strong by first entering the sanctuary of the soul, where they will be protected from all the world's terror and tumult by our unconquerable Majestic King, who is enthroned there.

Such souls do not see the saddest part of it. They have become so used to their struggle, so used to dealing with the vermin that attack the outer walls of the castle that they actually become just like these foul things! If they are attacked by anger, they fasten all attention on their attacker and become strong and aggressive themselves—rather than learning how to defeat a hostile enemy by patient humility, as our Lord directed (Matthew 5:38–47). Thinking that they are resisting in spirit, for the Lord's sake, they resist in the flesh and lose their way.

And so, though they have been created with a nature that is richly endowed with the ability to commune in spirit with God himself—yet there is no healing and no rest for them. These souls are like Lot's wife. Though they are told very simply to turn away from spiritual oppression, and from external destruction of every terrible kind—though their way of escape is to flee to spiritual safety in the Lord—they fail to do so.

Therefore, they miss the very path that would lead them to spiritual victory over the world and, like Lot's wife, they are changed into useless pillars of salt. Bemoaning their poor fate, they are powerless to accomplish the Lord's will, which is to lead others to spiritual victory over the world and to himself (Matthew 5:13–16).

I have explained all this in order to bring you to the head of the spiritual path—and that is prayer. I mean both vocal prayer, by which we speak out simple needs, and the prayer of meditation, by which we behold with the eyes of our soul the One who is Lord over all.

Here we begin.

THE INTERIOR CASTLE

My Ever-present Father, I hear your loving and holy call. And I want to stop my asking, bargaining, and demanding.

Today, I let go of all I'm struggling to hold on to. Open my eyes to the answers and the miracles that I want . . . more than I want you.

Right now, I want to be still and to know your presence.

34

4
"You Know the Way. . . ."

Jesus said, "In my Father's house are many rooms. . . . You know the way. . . ." Thomas said to him, "Lord, we don't know where you are going, so how can we know the way?"

John 14:2, 4–5

Jesus said to them, "In . . . patience, possess ye your souls."

Luke 21:19, KJV

He who rules his spirit [is greater] than he who takes a city.

Proverbs 16:32, RSV

Our souls were created in the image and likeness of God. . . .

How unfortunate that we do not really

35

understand ourselves. We are blind to who we really are, and even the blindness is our own fault.

Suppose an otherwise normal man was asked, "Who is your father? Who is your mother? What country are you from?" And suppose his reply was, "I have no idea." Wouldn't we think this man was absurdly ignorant?

But isn't our spiritual ignorance just as absurd? So many Christians of "strong faith" make no attempt to discover their true identity in relation to our King. Most are so preoccupied with worldly pastimes they are only vaguely aware of the needs of their physical body, let alone the hunger and thirst of their spirit!

Our faith tells us we can "possess our souls." Those few who would think on this matter at all might say, "I assume that I *do* possess my soul." They do not see the evidence that they rule over their souls, however, and they do not even know how they may do so.

That is because we so seldom consider the nature or quality of our inner life. We do not see Who it is that dwells within us. We do not know the spiritual treasure that it is to enjoy communion with Him. And so we make little effort to guard or nurture the soul's beauty. All of our attention is focused on the externals—not only the outward needs of the body, but the outward demonstrations of our faith, as well. So we focus on the outer walls of the castle, while within, the treasures of heaven lie in waste.

You would do well to imagine that in this castle are many "mansions" or rooms (John 14:2). Some are above, some below, and others to the sides. But in the *center*. . . !

In the center is the main dwelling place. Here, we may stand in the clear light of God, knowing ourselves as we truly are, and known of God at the same time. Here, the most intimate exchanges may take place between God and the soul.

If you keep this comparison always in mind— that of a castle with a wondrous throne within— God may use it to draw you into His presence, where He bestows the favors that He loves to grant. . . .

THE INTERIOR CASTLE

My only True Father, sometimes when I think of the spiritual progress I've made, I hear accusing voices. . . . I see my failures and sins. . . . Still you remain true to me.

Thank you that you have opened the way, by the life and the blood of Jesus, for me to come before your throne . . . as a treasured child.

5
Unstable

If anyone lacks wisdom [on how to persevere and become mature in spirit] he should ask God, who gives generously to all without finding fault, and it will be given to him. But when he asks, he must believe and not doubt, because he who doubts is like a wave of the sea, blown and tossed by the wind.

James 1:5, 6, KJV

For most of my early life I did not travel the path of true prayer, which sifts the heart. And so for nearly twenty years, I lived as one driven before gale winds, constantly thrown by one storm after another. The way of prayer could have been a strong pillar for me to lean on, against all storms inward and outward, but I did not understand it then.

So, I look back on that part of my life as the most painful time one can imagine. Though I was a Christian, I had no peace or rest, none of the inward sweetness that comes from God. And of course there is no sweetness in circumstances, which are changeable, nor from people, who are unreliable. And certainly there was no sweetness in my sins, which seemed inescapable.

I shed many tears for my faults, and always ended in angry frustration at myself. Yet nothing kept me from failing again and again, not even my remorseful tears. The first real step toward freedom came only when I saw that even honest remorse was little more than a delusion.

It was the Lord, in His rich goodness, who gave me the deeper prick of conscience that was needed. He awakened me to a truer, deeper view of my unruly soul. And He was most gracious to give me this insight before I had reformed.

I saw, at last, that the root of evil's hold upon me lay in my *will*. For I had not been willing to avoid every occasion for sin. Yes, I was spiritual in my way of *thinking* and even in my outward *actions*—but in my inmost heart I was divided because of doubt, fixing my heart on the life and the treasures of this world.

I must add, as a warning to you, that my spiritual counselors did not help me very much to escape this double-mindedness. No one saw, or even understood, what a dangerous path my heart was traveling on. No one told me that we must learn to see each place where our will is at odds with the will of our Lord.

The Lord made me to see clearly: I could employ my will to turn away from every occasion for sin. I became aware of every attempt my rebellious soul was making, seeking its ultimate happiness in people, in peaceful circumstances, and in earthly possessions.

If someone had helped me to see this—how to repent and change from the heart—I believe my misery would have ended more quickly.

All during those years, God was so patient and loving with me. I still had the courage to pray—I say *courage* because nothing in the whole world requires more courage than to plot treason against our Majestic King, *knowing* that He knows our plot, and still daring to enter His presence in prayer!

All that time I had been struggling to reconcile my weak life in God with a heart so rooted in sin.

I know now that God understood I was blind on this matter, and being led by blind guides as well. . . . I say this so those who read my words will see how gracious God is as He works with each of us, wayward souls that we are. It is He who gives the courage to continue praying, even when we harbor many rebellions in our hearts and continually turn back to our sins.

If the soul perseveres with this courage, seeking God himself—in spite of sin and temptation and lapses into spiritual coldness—He comes to our aid. He will guide such a soul to the place where we see that our *only safety* is in Him, who is our promised salvation. . . .

I assure you, then, from hard experience: Never stop seeking God in prayer, no matter how

41

miserable and failing you are at this moment.
Prayer is the way to open ourselves to God, and
the way in which He shows us our unstable
hearts and begins to strengthen them. When you
are tempted to give up on prayer—as you surely
will be—thinking you are too bad to change, it is
the voice of the Devil who never gives up trying
to keep us separated from God.

If you find yourself in this spiritual state—
feeling wayward, unstable in heart, confused as
to why you are not growing and changing in the
Lord—I say this: Keep turning from sin, and
cling to the Lord in prayer!

He always hears, and He will answer.

THE LIFE OF THERESA OF JESUS

*My Father—my soul's Strength, you
know that on my own I will fail in walking with you.*

*When my earthly strengths fail . . . When spiritual
friends and my understanding of your Word are not
enough . . . draw me from doubt . . . more deeply into
you. Steady me, Father.*

6
Seek, and Be Strong

No eye has seen, no ear has heard, no mind has conceived what God has prepared for those who love him—but God has revealed it to us by his Spirit.

1 Corinthians 2:9–10

March on, my soul; be strong!

Judges 5:21

God longs to give favor—that is, spiritual strength and health—to those who seek Him, and Him alone. He grants spiritual favors and victories, not because the one who seeks Him is holier than anyone else, but in order to make His holy beauty and His great redeeming power known. . . . For it is through the living witness of others that we are drawn to God at all. It is because of His creatures, and His work in them, that we come to praise Him.

But there are many who say, "It is not wise to speak about such matters. After all, seeking God in such a pure and single-minded way is impossible. All it does is make weak believers feel frustrated and embarrassed."

My response is this: It is a far greater loss to stop telling Christians there is a higher life in the Spirit—greater wonders in God!

We should never stop seeking out the ones on whom God bestows spiritual strength. Nor should we stop listening to or honoring such people, because we can learn from them how to walk with God more closely.

If only we would listen *more closely* to the spiritual wisdom of such people—and not to the doubters! Then we would understand God and His desires more clearly, and we would fall in love with Him. For He is, indeed, a wonderful Father who longs to pour out His mercy upon us, and whose majesty is so great that He can transform us from deep within.

. . . If anyone does not believe that God longs to give greater evidences of His transforming love, then of course they will never seek Him in this way, never find Him in actual living experience. Our Lord desires—*passionately desires!*—never to have His work in you held back by ignorance or unbelief.

Therefore, do not let this type of limiting unbelief stand in your way.

THE INTERIOR CASTLE

My Father, my soul's Friend—reach for me today with your strong arm.

Today, I fix my eyes only upon you. I declare the wonder that I see: My high and holy God . . . humbling yourself . . . choosing death on a cross . . . rising in power . . . so I can share in your spiritual might.

7
Set Your Heart

Since . . . you have been raised with Christ, set your hearts on things above. . . . Set your minds on things above, not on earthly things. For you died, and your life is now hidden with Christ in God.

Colossians 3:1–3

Be imitators of God . . . as dearly loved children and live a life of love, just as Christ loved us and gave himself up for us. . . .

Ephesians 5:1–2

The kingdom of God is . . . righteousness, peace and joy in the Holy Spirit, because anyone who serves Christ in this way is pleasing to God and approved by men.

Romans 14:17, 18

I spent more than fourteen years without being able to meditate upon the Lord, except while I was reading the Scriptures or devotional writings.

There are many people like this . . . those who find their thoughts wandering so much they cannot concentrate upon one thing. Those people are plagued with a restless soul.

Therefore, when they try to fix their thoughts upon God, they are attacked by a thousand foolish distractions. Or they wind up fretting over their sins and failures in scrupulous detail—and so they spend all their time fixed upon themselves and wonder why their times of devotion are so unpleasant. And of course all manner of doubts rush in upon the restless soul. . . .

There are many who are seeking to grow in faith, yet when they fail to sense God's consoling presence, they assume there is some fault in themselves. They become anxious about their own faith and even their salvation. They take their eyes off the Lord and try to imitate the example of others. If, for example, they see someone weeping over their sins, they worry if perhaps they are not sorry enough about their own failures, worried that perhaps they are not shedding "enough tears." They wrongly conclude that if they were better servants of God, they would be weeping all the time. . . . Do not mistake me, tears are good, but only when they are genuine, spilling from a contrite heart (Psalm 51:17).

We must learn to follow the spiritual path without being sidetracked, which we can be by outward shows of piety and fervent emotion (Matthew 6:1–18). There is greater peace and safety in these spiritual practices, by which the heart follows higher things and is changed into the image of Christ:

Humility—that is, the attitude of heart that peacefully rests in God, receiving all things as from His good hands, so that we may have joy in Him no matter what our circumstances (Philippians 4:4–7).

Mortification—which means allowing God to reveal and put to death the worldly attitude in us that seeks esteem and power over others, so that we can freely love God and affectionately serve others, in all meekness (1 John 2:16).

Detachment—that is, letting go of all our earthly "securities," whether possessions or people, and to trust only in our Lord, whose kingdom is eternal! (John 18:36; Romans 14:17, 18).

There are other spiritual virtues that we may learn to practice. If we pursue them, then we need not fear that we will fail to walk in greater and greater spiritual perfection, like those who deeply contemplate God and know Him and imitate Him.

THE WAY OF PERFECTION

My Father—*You are worthy of my all!
Yet the compass needle of my heart is so often drawn by
a need for earthly security, human attention, and
admiration.*

*Show me that my first need is to know you as you
are—in your love, in the beauty of your holiness, and
in your righteous correction.*

Correct my course.

The Friends of God

*T*he Lord disciplines those he loves, as a father
[disciplines] the son he delights in.

Proverbs 3:12

*F*aithful are the wounds of a friend; profuse are the
kisses of an enemy.

Proverbs 27:6, RSV

I wrote you [about the terrible, open sin among you]
out of great distress and anguish of heart and with
many tears, not to grieve you but to let you know the
depth of my love for you. . . . I wrote . . . to see if
you would stand the test and be obedient in
everything.

2 Corinthians 2:4, 9

*S*piritual love will always be a reflection of

the love that is shown to us by Jesus, the Good Lover. . . .

The heart of one who loves as Jesus loves cannot practice duplicity. If they see a friend straying from the spiritual path or trapped by sins, they cannot help themselves—they will speak to their friend at once, with gentleness and humility, hoping to help them back into the way of life!

What if the friend does not accept the correction, and does not correct the problem? The one who loves with God's love will not flatter, or hide anything from his friend, no matter how difficult it may be to say. For the one whose course is set to follow God will feel torn inside, at war with his friend—and the error will either be corrected, or there will be a parting of ways. . . .

You should be very happy if you are given a friend who loves you in this way—that is, a friend who wants to see you progress in spirit and become more like Christ. You should thank God for the day you met a person who is like this, for those are rare indeed.

Oh, Lord, I ask that you grant me this favor: Give me such friends, who care for my spiritual progress and are not afraid to oppose me when necessary. Truly, Lord, I would rather have this gift of godly friendship than to be loved by all the powerful rulers of this world!

A godly friend will do everything in his power to help us escape all worldly entanglements, so that we can be free to rule over everything! . . .

Getting to know the ones who are, first and last, God's friends is a very good way of "having" Him at your side. . . . For, under the Lord, it is because of people like this that I am not in hell.

THE WAY OF PERFECTION

My Loving Father, I confess to you that, most often, I'm irritated by correction. I react by struggling to defend myself, and my soul is left feeling wounded and in turmoil.

Today, open my eyes to see your hand of correction—even through the one who criticizes me unfairly. Thank you that you can help me to escape my pride . . . and to see beyond the one who corrects me . . . to receive all correction as training from your hand of love.

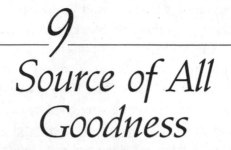

Source of All Goodness

Every good and perfect gift is from above, coming down from the Father of the heavenly lights . . . but the man who looks intently into the perfect law that gives freedom and continues to do this, not forgetting what he has heard but doing it—*he will be blessed. . . .*

James 1:17, 25 (emphasis added)

Your attitude should be the same as that of Christ Jesus: Who . . . humbled himself. . . .

Philippians 2:5, 6, 8

I know a person who discovered a secret that helped her to grow greatly in the image of Christ. She learned how to use a spiritual "mirror," as it were, and I must tell you its use and its great benefit.

This woman knew that the *good* we do never

originates in us, but rather it is a reflection of goodness from whatever bright source we behold with the eyes of the soul. She knew that it is this Sun, this light of greater goodness, which warms us and causes us to grow in goodness. She saw clearly that in ourselves there is no good thing (Romans 7:18). Therefore, any good deed that she did, and any good done by another, originated with God, who is our sole source of Goodness. In this way, she came to understand that there is an active principle behind these words of our Lord: "Apart from me, you can do nothing" (John 15:5).

This brings us to the first room we will come to as we proceed within the interior castle of our souls. I am referring to the room of *self-knowledge*. If you want to journey toward God on safe and level footing—pay attention to this warning! Do not be distracted by other spiritual "methods" which falsely promise you that you can "fly"! Self-knowledge is painful and it requires effort, but it is the right room in which to start.

It is my firm opinion that we can never know ourselves—that is, we cannot know our heart's secret motives—unless we seek to look into the face of God. And so *He* is the One we must look to, fixing our eyes on His utter goodness. In this sense, He becomes our spiritual "mirror": By gazing into His majesty—seeing that He came from so high and stooped so low—we become aware of how opposite we are to His nature. We seek earthly heights, and we sin against others to get our way, and so we prove what low creatures we are.

Here is our first glimpse in the mirror, then: As we gaze into the face of Him who is so pure, we will at once see how corrupt we are.

Let us meditate long on His great, lovely humility that we may see how far we have strayed from following on the low path our Master walks.

THE INTERIOR CASTLE

My Good Father, I thank you that you sent Jesus to reflect your light . . . and your Spirit to replace my evil with your goodness. I recommit my life, today, to fulfill your will here on earth as it is done in heaven.

And I commit into your hands the people I love, and all the circumstances of their lives . . . even those I don't think of now as good.

10
Throne of Grace

Jesus said, "The kingdom of God is within you."

Luke 17:21

Enter his gates with thanksgiving and his courts with praise. . . .

Psalm 100:4

Let us . . . approach the throne of grace with confidence. . . .

Hebrews 4:16

Consider what your Master, Jesus, prayed when He taught us to say, "Our Father, *who art in heaven . . .*"

Why is it that most believers have so little concern to know about the realm of heaven? After all, it is the realm where our most holy Father dwells. Doesn't it make sense, then, that we should want to know how to *walk the paths of* His spiritual kingdom?

I tell you, it is most urgent that you learn the sure way to walk with the Lord. Certainly, your own thoughts will not lead you there, because left to their natural pathways they merely wander whenever you pray, and lead you nowhere.

But when we learn about the realm of heaven—I tell you that your whole understanding suddenly comes into focus, and your scattered soul is recollected so that you experience a wonderful unity of spirit! Let us go on then.

You already know that God is everywhere (Psalm 139). Clearly, where the court has been built, the King is in residence. And where God is, there is heaven—*heaven!* where His Majesty reigns in glory.

Now I would ask you to think on the words of Augustine. He sought God in many places and finally discovered that he could not find God outside of himself but *within* himself. Once a struggling and anxious soul learns this truth, it is life to your very bones—that we do not need to search for heaven, over here or over there, in order to find our eternal Father. In fact, we do not even need to speak out loud, for though we speak in the smallest whisper or the most fleeting thought *He is close enough to hear us.*

. . . We need only to find a quiet place without distractions, and to still our loud and rambling thoughts . . . and then we will behold Him, in His courts, deep within our souls.

. . . The throne on which He sits—a throne

of immense value—is your very *heart*. . . .

Do you see the wonderful mystery of it all?—That He who could fill a thousand worlds and more by His greatness is so great that He can confine himself in such small space. . . . That He, being sovereign Lord, longs to bring us liberty. And that He, whose love for us is so high, has lowered himself to enter our nature.

And this you should know, too. When a soul begins to comprehend God, He does not reveal himself fully, all at once. Otherwise, the soul would be overwhelmed at being so "small," so petty a place—yet it is the royal court of so great a God. Therefore, a little at a time, God enlarges our soul's capacity to comprehend Him, as He sees the need to do so. . . .

I tell you this so that you will give yourself to Him—relinquish yourself totally to Him! Resolve that you will allow Him to do whatever He wants with your life. This will bring His Majesty great pleasure in you, and He has His own reasons why this type of surrendered life must be so in this present age. Do not be afraid or refuse Him the right to take you and shape you in any way He chooses (Isaiah 29:16; 64:8).

He will not force us, He will only take what we give to Him. Know this, though—He does not give himself to us fully until we fully give ourselves to Him.

THE WAY OF PERFECTION

61

My Father of Grace, your greatness and beauty are higher than my mind can think or imagine . . . greater than any earthly thing that weighs me down today.

Right now, I come into your presence with praise . . . knowing the power of your grace can transform every bitter thing into sweetness . . . can change even the most difficult challenge into my means of spiritual victory over this world.

11
Choose Love

*Jesus . . . took off his outer clothing, and wrapped a
towel around his waist . . . and began to wash his
disciples' feet. . . . Jesus said, "A new command I give
you. . . . As I have loved you, so you must
love one another."*

John 13:3–5, 34

Do not fear that I am going to direct you to
begin many different spiritual practices and
disciplines in order to walk more closely with
God. With the Lord's help, though, I hope that
you will begin to walk in the way that pleases
Him.

To do so, I suggest only that we choose the
spiritual practices that our early Church fathers
practiced, and which they directed us to follow. It
is a serious mistake to look for another spiritual
path to follow, or to try to learn how to live in the
spirit from anyone who has not learned the right
practices, those which have been handed down to
us.

One of these "practices" is to make a wholehearted commitment to love each other. . . .

Love is of utmost importance. Once you have set your will that you will learn the way of love, then there is no flaw or irritation in another person that you cannot bear. You will find, in fact, that you are able to live so at peace that it will take a truly exceptional irritation to affect your love for anyone.

If this one commandment were kept—"Love one another"—I know that it would carry us a long way toward keeping all the rest of our Lord's commands.

THE WAY OF PERFECTION

My Father—Shaper of my soul, I know that this one word, "love," is a command that will break and refashion me . . . if I let it.

From this day on, I ask you to take me to the heights and the depths of that one command.

12
God, Just and True

Jesus replied: "Love the Lord your God with all your heart and with all your soul and with all your mind." This is the first and greatest commandment.

Matthew 22:37, 38

Oh, how I love your law! I meditate on it all day long . . . therefore I hate every wrong path.

Psalm 119:97, 104

And I saw [in heaven] what looked like a sea of glass mixed with fire and, standing beside the sea, those who had been victorious over the beast . . . and [they] sang the song of Moses. . . . "Just and true are your ways, King of the ages!"

Revelation 15:2–3

Our natural way is so unstable. We love

some people too much, and we love others far too little, and some not at all. And so we reel to one side or the other, and stagger off the path of God's perfect love (1 Corinthians 13).

There are some who do not understand God's love, however, and they think it means always to be nice and never to be severe. Anyone who has ever seen this kind of "love" in action knows that it leads to this: It wrongly allows room for imperfections, which only grow and lead to greater evil. Many snares are set by the devil along this way.

The soul that is set to love God first, though, will see through the pretty veneer of this type of "love."

If you love God first, you are free to face any rugged encounter in your relationship with another—whether it is their anger or rejection or tears—in order to bring that beloved one to freedom in the truth. Those who have not set their consciences to please God first seldom walk so risky a path with another because they know they might be attacked, and that threatens their love of self! So they say only niceties, and deceive themselves into thinking they are virtuous.

But those who are seeking to love God perfectly do not want to be "spared" from the truth. And they will seek to grow strong in the love of God, so that they may wisely speak the truth to others, as well.

Otherwise, little by little, we will slowly

deprive our wills of the strength they need—that is, the strength to live lives that are given wholly and entirely in the love of God.

My Father, Just and Fair, make me to love your justice so that I can overcome the plans of the wicked one . . . and be free from the sins that want to trip me up.

Help me to accept that if . . . I allow you to lead me through opposition or hardship . . . if I accept even hard words that challenge . . . you will work your righteous life into me.

13
Come Swiftly, Spirit

Make every effort to enter that rest [in God]. . . . For the word of God is living and active. Sharper than any double-edged sword, it penetrates to dividing even soul and spirit, joints and marrow; it judges the thoughts and attitudes of the heart. Nothing in all creation is hidden from God's sight.

Hebrews 4:11–13

[True] circumcision is circumcision of the heart, by the Spirit. . . .

Romans 2:29

Seeking to live a spiritual life while staying in close contact with the world is no easy matter. If you think so, you are dangerously mistaken.

We live in the world, and we have to do business with the world. Because of their work or position, some must even live as worldly men do, taking part in the luxuries of this world. Yet *inwardly* we are strangers to the world and enemies of its way of thinking and its false system of honor. For at this present time, we are living in exile from our true home—and so we must abide in two worlds, living like men and women, but thinking and acting like angels!

. . . If we would lead others, with spiritual wisdom and insight, we must live inwardly as men and women who see ourselves protected as in a mighty fortress.

Our first rampart is this: to understand that nothing this world offers is eternal or lasting, and nothing earthly can offer the hope or security of knowing life eternal. In fact, earthly things can transfix us, trap us, keep us from forsaking all in order to know God. If you come to see things this way, you will keep this world and all its alluring offers from having any power over your spirit.

This is the manner by which we become *detached* from the things of this earth—whether people, or possessions, or honored positions. And this detachment is a great good, because all these things, great or lovely as they may seem, will come to an end. We need to let them go, and become *attached* to things eternal.

If we do not learn to live within our spiritual fortress, we will betray ourselves sooner or later and let the enemy within our walls.

. . . Do not think for a moment this is a small matter. Do not think that the type of spiritual life

I am telling you about can be achieved quickly or in an easy way. No, indeed we need a great deal of God's empowering grace. For this is a spiritual battle we have entered. I am speaking of the battle between the world and the spirit—the battle for our very souls.

THE WAY OF PERFECTION

My Father—my soul's Fortress, come with your swift sword . . . and divide my soul's self-righteous or legalistic efforts from my spirit's longing to draw Life from you.

I hide myself in the righteousness of your Son. I let go of my efforts to justify and defend myself.

Today, I will stand . . . only in you.

14
Father, Keep Me

Keep your servant also from willful sins; may they not rule over me. Then will I be blameless, innocent of great transgression.

Psalm 19:13

The man who says, "I know [God]," but does not do what he commands is a liar, and the truth is not in him . . . Whoever claims to live in him must walk as Jesus did.

1 John 1:5–6

*T*urn the eyes of your understanding once more to this beautiful sight—to the splendid castle of your soul. It is the place where the King comes to reign on His throne, and so it shines with the brilliance of a pearl from the treasures of the Far East. It is from the soul, when it is rooted in God, that you find deep, true life. And so your soul is also like a tree, planted in the midst of the waters of Life (Psalm 1:3).

What a tragedy it is for those who understand this spiritual path—and then plunge themselves back into darkness by choosing to turn back to their sin, which gave them no life to begin with! There is no night so black, no pathway so obscured and lost, as when this happens.

You must see it this way: The Sun himself has given the palace of your soul all its beauty and radiance, and it is true that He always remains at the center of your soul. And yet, when we choose to turn back to sin and worldliness it is as if He were not there at all, so far as our soul's interaction and communion with Him are concerned. The soul is still as *capable* of enjoying Him as a crystal is of catching the sunlight.

Nothing we do when we are in such a state is of any spiritual profit. Do not be deceived: When we have willingly turned back to sin, the "good works" we do are only attempts to cover over our sin, or to show God and others we are still good. They are of no use, and win us only shame and not glory. For sin separates us from the outpouring of grace, and this is grace: the presence of God himself, who is the source of all-powerful Goodness.

So when we separate ourselves from Him, we cut ourselves off from our source of goodness—so how can we please Him in any way?

Train yourselves to see things in this way: When we choose sin over God's goodness, we are walking within the dark purpose of the devil,

who is darkness incarnate. No wonder then that
our poor souls seem swallowed in darkness. . . .

THE INTERIOR CASTLE

*My Father—my Good Shepherd, show
me my small but willful sins . . . all the times I allow
myself to wander—just a little here, a little there—
while I think I'm walking in your Light.*

15
New Wine

[My lover] has taken me to the banquet hall, and his banner over me is love. . . . "Drink your fill, O lovers."

Song of Songs 2:4; 5:1

Jesus spoke to them again in parables, saying: "The kingdom of heaven is like a king who prepared a wedding banquet for his son. . . . But [many] paid no attention. . . ."

Matthew 22:1–2, 5

Do you suppose that the Lord would admit people who are only lovers of pleasure into His close friendship? Or people who want only to live free of trials? Such a thought is ridiculous.

I am sure now that God gives His closest friends much greater trials than anyone else! He leads them by the most difficult and rugged road, and sometimes they feel as though they are completely lost. Sometimes they even think they must know nothing about God or His ways, and that they are spiritual infants who need to go back to the simplest lessons of faith and begin all over again.

But let me assure you of this: His Majesty does not want them to turn back to the beginnings of their faith—but to press deeper. If they are willing to go into the depths with Him, He obliges himself to give them spiritual nourishment to strengthen their souls—not sips of water, as you would give to a thirsty child, but delicious wine of the Spirit!

When this happens, it is as if they are made drunk by the Spirit, so that they are hardly affected by the pain they are going through and they are capable of bearing it. Thus, the man or woman who knows how to deeply contemplate the utter goodness and love of our Lord is strong and courageous.

A person whose spirit is on this path cannot be shaken from serving the Lord no matter how great their suffering. For if they come to Him in their weakness, the Lord immediately lifts them in spirit by giving a strong drink of inner courage, so they have no fear whatsoever, no matter what sort of trial they are facing.

. . . For the one who does not know how, thus, to walk in the Spirit with the Lord—well, I do not see that they would be able to endure

78

the same sort of trials for even a day without betraying the Lord.

THE WAY OF PERFECTION

Your Majesty, Lord of the Banquet!— give me a drink of this new wine . . . the wine of your presence. Let the world fade, and sharpen my senses to you.

16
Works From the Heart

*We are God's workmanship, created in Christ Jesus
to do good works, which God prepared in advance
for us to do.*

Ephesians 2:10

*The Lord declares, "Why spend . . . your labor on
what does not satisfy?"*

Isaiah 55:2

The Lord knows every one of us as we really are.

The Lord is the one who gives us our spiritual callings, and our daily work to do. He chooses for us, according to what He knows will be best for our souls, what will be best for His purposes, and what will be best for our neighbors whom we are to serve.

Have you sought the Lord about the work you

are to do for Him? Have you, then, prepared yourself to do it, obediently? If so, then you have no need to fear that your life's efforts will be lost.

Strive to know and be faithful in the work the Lord has for you to do in this life according to His purpose. For we are here, in this life, for no other reason.

But do not think that you can leave off your search to know His purpose for you after you've sought Him on this matter for a year or two—or even after ten years! If we do so, we are abandoning our true work of faith like cowards— for our work is to be always and only obedient, no matter where He leads us. It is well and good that the Lord should see we are not willing to leave anything undone that He wants us to accomplish in this life.

Think of yourself as a good soldier. No matter how long and how well you have served, you must always remain at ready for your Captain to send you away on any assignment he would entrust to you. Remember who it is who will issue your "pay"—and remember that His payment is far, far superior to anything offered by people in this world!

Remember, too, that when our Captain sees you are present and eager to serve Him, He will assign you duties that are perfectly suited to you.

So never give up your habit of prayer. Never stop speaking to Him, and listening for Him. For the Lord is dearer to each one of us than the likeness of a captain would imply—He is your Spouse, and you never know when He shall call you.

THE WAY OF PERFECTION

My Father—Creator, *forgive me when I focus only on the "big goals" for my life . . . on my accomplishments and my own plans.*

Open my eyes, today, to see how I can serve you by serving the people you have placed in my life . . . in the acts of love, kindness, and peace you have prepared for me to do.

17
No Taste for Prayer

I was senseless and ignorant; I was like a brute beast before you. Yet I am always with you; you hold me by my right hand. You guide me with your counsel, and afterward you will take me into glory.

Psalm 73:22–24 (emphasis added)

Jesus said, "Your Father knows what you need before you ask him. This, then, is how you should pray: Our Father . . . your kingdom come, your will be done. . . ."

Matthew 6:8–10

For many years, I spent my daily hour of prayer struggling against one underlying wish—*to see the hour end.* I would actually pray while watching the hourglass. Even worse, I would feel such a heaviness of spirit as I dragged myself to the chapel where I prayed that I often had to force myself to go inside at all. Looking back, I can see how the Lord was helping me all the way, reluctant as I was.

But it is important for you to know this fact: I found greater spiritual stability, peace, and unshakable happiness when I trained myself to pray, even when I was reluctant, than I found from the times when I experienced excitement and emotional "rapture" in prayer.

If my Lord put up with me so long—indeed, He carried me through—while I was being such a wicked and unwilling servant, no one else need despair, no matter how wickedly unwilling they may be. For I received so many blessings from the Lord, and I felt so much of His empowering grace during all that time—surely no one else has been given more help than I! How ironic that I remained stubborn and resistant so long, when prayer was the very means by which God gave me inner nourishment and peace and joy, and I *knew* it.

I will say this again so you will not miss the point: Prayer was the one true door through which I met with the Lord in spirit, and through which He entered my soul to give me all-sustaining grace—and He gave, and gave, and gave freely all those years.

But prayer mixed with *trust* . . . now that was another matter.

I would pray for help over and over again, it is true. But I made a mistake all that time, which deadened my poor efforts. I did not place my whole trust in His Majesty. Oh, that I had totally and utterly distrusted my *self*—but I did not. If only I had despised and suspected the conniving, secretly clinging *self* hidden within me.

Yes, I certainly did seek help from the Lord during all those years. But I did not understand: It is of little use to seek God's help until we root out every bit of confidence we place in ourselves—in our opinions, our understanding, our personal strengths.

Our prayers are pathetic, indeed, until we place all confidence, once and forever, absolutely, in God.

Until I saw my mistake, those were the most miserable eighteen years of my life. . . .

THE LIFE OF THERESA OF JESUS

My Father—my Sovereign Majesty, so often I come to you, asking you to bless my plans, asking you to act as I see fit. No wonder you do not answer . . . and my prayers are dry.

Convict me, Father, when I commit this treason— of attempting to sit upon your throne and to govern my life in your place.

18
Pure in Heart

The little foxes . . . ruin the vineyards. . . .

Song of Songs 2:15

Jesus . . . gave them authority over evil spirits.

Mark 6:6–7

Create in me a pure heart, O God, and renew a steadfast spirit within me.

Psalm 51:10

I often reflect about the mistake parents make when they do not train their children in terms of right and wrong—that is, in terms of godly standards.

My own mother was, as I have said before, a very good woman. Nevertheless, when I was old enough to think for myself and to evaluate right and wrong, I did not derive as much spiritual good from her as I could have—in fact, I derived almost nothing at all.

Rather, she did little to train me in spiritual understanding, and because of that I learned that it was all right to be undisciplined in terms of spiritual standards and godly habits. Spiritually, this did me much harm.

My mother was fond of reading very romantic novels about chivalrous knights and great ladies. This pastime did her no spiritual harm, as far as I can tell, because she never absorbed herself so deeply in it that it distracted her from other duties and good practices. But it harmed me a great deal. As her children, we were free to read all of the same books. In Mother's defense, she may have allowed herself this distraction to take her mind off her own physical suffering, which was great. And she may have allowed us the same distraction, thinking it would keep us from doing worse things!

There was also the matter of my father: He was greatly annoyed by these books and thought them worthless—and we developed the wrong habit of concealing them from him so he would not know what we were reading.

In this way, I concentrated all my attentions on these books, and read them hungrily. Looking back, this little fault that I picked up from my mother was the beginning of spiritual lukewarmness. It eroded my better spiritual desires and pursuits, and it was the beginning of my falling away into worldliness in many respects.

At the time, of course, I thought nothing of wasting many hours, night and day, in reading such trivial and stupid books—even though it meant acting deceptively so as to keep a secret from my own father. I was so thoroughly mastered by my craving that I thought I would be miserable if I could not get my hands on the newest book.

All that flowery language, all those lovely, desirable ladies and gallant men—I began to become fussy and picky about my clothes, hungry to be pleasing in the eyes of others by means of my physical appearance. I took great pains with my hands and the styling of my hair, insisted on using only fine perfumes. I used every vanity within my grasp, until I was given over to utter worldliness.

You must see the real danger in all this: In all my vanities, I never dreamed I was doing evil to myself, because I never thought for a minute that someone like me—an everyday young woman— was driving God further from me by my total attention and dependence upon my outward appearance. It never occurred to me then.

All this fuss and obsession with my looks and mannerisms went on for many years. And there were many other practices that were not evil in themselves but, nonetheless, kept me from finding the true spiritual way. At the time, I did not see them as the least bit harmful.

Now I see perfectly well how wrong I was—

how cold and spiritually deadening these worldly
habits were.

THE LIFE OF THERESA OF JESUS

*My Father of all that is pure, make me
ready . . . and willing . . . to receive the order from
you today . . . to let go of corrupting things.*

*Let me blame no one else for my failing. Search me
and find the secret door in my soul that I leave open
. . . just a crack . . . for impurity and evil to crawl in.*

19
Reflections of Light

Put off your old self. . . . Do not let any unwholesome talk come out of your mouths, but only what is helpful for building up others according to their needs. . . . For you were once darkness, but now you are light in the Lord.

Ephesians 4:22, 29; 5:8

I learned a great many *little evils* from one of my cousins, who came to our house often. She was a silly and frivolous girl, and Mother took pains to keep us apart, for she seemed to have a sense that no good was rubbing off on me from her.

But Mother was not successful in blocking my cousin's visits, for there were so many legitimate reasons for her to come over.

I began to look forward to this girl's company, and loved to gossip and pass hours in idle talk with her. She encouraged me in all the vain pastimes I liked, and introduced me to many more I would never have thought of on my own.

I was fourteen at the time, and in my heart I never wanted to turn away from God in willful sin. I had a healthy fear of God. For this reason I never forfeited my personal reputation, as other girls my age were doing.

I failed to see, however, that I was failing God and failing myself in many other ways. I was extremely careful to keep my own honor intact—only because I was vain, and did not want to be spoken of as low or common. . . . But I was very clever whenever I did anything wrong, doing it in a way that others would not see.

Even then, young as I was, I was sometimes amazed at the evil this one wrong companion could bring into my life. The power of her words to influence me was so great—and I *allowed* myself to be influenced—so that I would find honor and acceptance in her eyes. . . . Let me be clear and say that the fault was not hers, it was mine. . . .

This is my point, though: Following this cousin, and another girl given to the same kind of amusements, I lost every trace of my soul's earlier inclination to seek good and high and sweet virtues. I lost myself and became merely a reflection of someone else.

From this terrible lost time, I know now the wonderful advantage it is, at any age, to have friends who are also seeking the good. I am certain that if, when I was young, I had been set among only good people, I would not have strayed from seeking a life of goodness and service to God. If I had found *anyone* to teach me about love and respect for God—that is, the healthy fear of the Lord—my tender spiritual resolves would have grown stronger, and I would never have fallen away.

But for a time, the fear of the Lord was blotted out by my soul's diversion into worldliness. My only fear was that someone would expose my sins and vanities and I would be dishonored—so I existed in a state of heightened self-love, and I was tormented all the time that I might be exposed and brought to shame.

THE LIFE OF THERESA OF JESUS, REVISION

My Father, I want to reflect your wonderful image in spirit—and not merely the attitudes and actions of people around me.

Free me from the opinions of others . . . and from self-love . . . so that I can become a clearer reflection of you.

20
New Spiritual Vision

Holy brothers, who share in the heavenly calling, fix your thoughts on Jesus, the apostle and high priest whom we confess . . . since the promise of entering his rest still stands, let us be careful that none of you be found to have fallen short of it . . . the message that [worldlings] heard was of no value to them, because those who heard did not combine it with faith.

Hebrews 3:1; 4:1–2

This is the victory that has overcome the world, even our faith.

1 John 5:4

When a person has done everything they can to detach themselves from the world . . . it would seem as if they have achieved a deep spirituality. One would think all their struggles are over.

Do not be fooled. Once you have seen the

need for living with a detached attitude toward this life—enjoying life, but not imprisoned by a false security in people or things—it only means that you have finally discovered a very, very important spiritual principle. Do not let yourself become smug or falsely secure with merely knowing the secret of detachment. Practice it. Otherwise you may fall asleep in your faith, and you will be like the man who climbs into his bed thinking he is safe because he has bolted all his doors and windows, when murderous thieves have already sneaked into his house.

And remember, when it comes to living and growing in the spiritual life, there is no worse thief than the one who lives in the house!

The battle will always be the same one, over and over again. Unless we take great care to watch what passes in our souls, we will fall into great deception. For the most important business of all is this: to set aside our self-will daily, moment by moment, and to live at peace in the will of our Lord.

Unless we make this transaction every day— that is, giving over our will to God—we will be prisoners to nearly everything in this world. Everything that goes against our will—and so many things do—will deprive us of the holy freedom in spirit that our souls so desperately crave. This is the faith that overcomes the world, for with this kind of freedom from the lead weights of earth, our souls are allowed to soar unburdened to their Maker.

It is a great help in laboring to achieve this sort of inner freedom and rest, if we keep one thought ready to use in our arsenal of spiritual weapons: Everything in this world is vain and will pass away!

I have found this a great weapon, which helps me free my affections from attachment to trivial things and to fix them on things that are eternal. No doubt, this will seem like poor help indeed to some, but if you try it you will see how quickly this places your soul within our eternal fortress.

Therefore, even in regards to "small" things, as soon as you find yourself growing too fond of them—that is, certain you cannot find security or happiness without them—forcefully withdraw your thoughts immediately! Then, set your thoughts upon God.

I know that His Majesty will help you to do this.

Our greatest work, which always seems to remain, is this: to become detached from our *selves*. It is a hard thing to detach from our selves enough to see our selves as we
really are—and even if we can do so, it is still a hard thing to oppose our selves . . . because our love for self is so dear, and so deadly.

THE WAY OF PERFECTION

My Father—*Giver of Spiritual Sight,*
I want to live free in you. Yet I seek security,
acceptance, and love in things of this world.

Show me the vanity—the sad futility—of placing
my faith in anything and anyone in this world . . .
which is weak and passing away. Open my eyes to the
enduring world of your Spirit.

Let my will, today, become one with yours.

21
The Garden of the Lord

The Lord will guide you always . . . in a sun-
scorched land [he] will strengthen your frame. You
will be like a well-watered garden. . . .

Isaiah 58:11

[God's] divine power has given us everything we
need for life and godliness . . . so that through them
you may participate in the divine nature. . . . For this
very reason, make every effort to add to your faith
goodness . . . knowledge . . . self-control . . .
perseverance . . . godliness . . . brotherly kindness
. . . love. For if you possess these qualities in
increasing measure, they will keep you from being
ineffective and unproductive. . . .

2 Peter 1:3, 4, 5–8

When you enter into the spiritual life
through the gateway of prayer, you would do

101

well to see yourself as one who has set out to create a garden.

This garden is a place wherein our Lord wants to come and walk and to take pleasure. But just now, the soil is barren—except for the places that produce clots of weeds. His Majesty wants to uproot the weeds and plant in this garden many fruitful and fragrant and blossoming plants. You may take it for granted that the Lord is already afoot, walking in His garden, if you have had any desire to seek Him in prayer, for He always calls to us first and it is His voice we hear when we think it is our desire to pray.

If we want to be good gardeners of this new-sown soul, we must, with God's help, see to it that the good plantings are tended and grow—and I am speaking now of the godly virtues. At very least, we must see that these good things are not neglected and die. Rather, we tend our souls carefully so that the first blossoms appear.

These are the spiritual "fragrances" that begin to rise from our lives—the fragrances of faith, goodness, self-control, love, and the like. By them, many, many others are refreshed in spirit and attracted to the Lord (2 Corinthians 2:14–16).

Then our Lord himself comes to walk in the midst of our garden. And it is all our joy to sense that He is there, taking pleasure in these lovely virtues.

THE LIFE OF THERESA OF JESUS

My Father, Gardener of my soul, today and in the days to come, begin to show me the attitudes and dispositions that you want to root out of me.

Begin to plant in me your character so that my soul is becoming a garden of sweet fragrances that attract others to you.

22
Rebels

Jesus said, "My kingdom is not of this world . . . my kingdom is from another place."

John 18:36

Jesus said, "The kingdom of heaven is like treasure hidden in a field. When a man found it . . . he went and sold all he had and bought that field."

Matthew 13:44

Lord of my soul, I know that from ages past to all eternity you are our highest Good! Yet, there is one matter I pondered for a long time: When someone firmly decides to follow you with all his heart, why is it that you do not instantly place your perfect love in that soul? Why do you not place within it your perfect peace, so that it will never want to wander from you again?

And now I know that you, in your kindness, overlook all questions like this, because they are asked out of blind ignorance. Once our hearts are flooded with your spiritual wisdom, we understand that we are at fault in the matter and not you.

Here lies the problem: We may pray day after day and petition you for all manner of things, thinking we are faithful in our prayers. But we have begun our spiritual journey at the wrong place. You long to set up your eternal dominion within our hearts. But rebels that we are, we are slow to trust you, and in our selfishness and fear we do not easily give over to you the central place in our souls—which is our heart's throne. I am speaking of our *will*.

So we continue to live as men and women who call you our King, but do not honor you as King with the tribute due to you. And you do not permit us to enjoy the sense of your presence when we will not pay the cost for so great a possession.

There is only one thing in the whole world that we can offer you, only one thing with which we "buy" the love of God, which you have promised to pour into our hearts by the Holy Spirit (Romans 5:5). The tribute you ask is that we love you deeply, and willingly give to you *all*—including the people we love, our belongings, our *selves*. Then we can begin our inward, spiritual rest in you, because we begin to act on the trust we so boldly tell others about—really trusting that you are always and only a Good Lord!

But instead we love the world, even when you tell us plainly through John, your friend and apostle, "Do not love the world or anything in the world" (1 John 2:15).

But if we take even the simplest, lame-footed steps toward you—if we stop clinging with our hearts to anything in this world, and set our treasure in heaven (Matthew 6:19–21)—then your kingdom floods into our hearts. And with it flows the river of peace and happiness of your presence, as many men and women of faith tell us. For you, my King, never withhold yourself from the man or woman who pays this price.

Now I know that to find this place in spirit, we must seek you steadfastly. And little by little you strengthen our souls, until we finally gain release from the chains of this world and live freely in your spiritual kingdom, where we know you reign (1 John 5:4).

This is the path of faith upon which a man or woman may set out. We will make great progress if we do enough violence to ourselves—that is, if we refuse to let our heart grasp for earthly securities. Then we win two victories. We will enter the kingdom of heaven ourselves and, because of our example, others will see the right way and will follow after us.

THE WAY OF PERFECTION

*P*atient Father, I ask you to declare war against my rebel heart—which wants to say that you are my King—while I violate the first law of your spiritual kingdom.

Give me courage, today, to let go of my hold on this failing world—and stand in you alone.

23
Worldliness

Jesus said again, "I am the gate; whoever enters through me will be saved. He will come in and go out, and find pasture."

John 10:7, 9

[Jesus'] disciples asked him what [the Parable of the Sower] meant. He said, . . . "The seed that fell among thorns stands for those who hear, but as they go on their way they are choked by life's worries, riches and pleasures, and they do not mature."

Luke 8:9, 10, 14

Consider what it is like for you when you try to enter into the castle of our King, which is within you.

Most of your days are totally absorbed with the affairs of this world. Yes, you have good *intentions*: You intend to pray and seek the Lord, you intend to grow in spirit—someday. Occasionally, you may even renew your

109

commitment to the Lord . . . but you will notice that these occasions become less and less frequent with time because, as you rightly note, they do not bring about lasting change or true spiritual growth.

All in all, most are very careless about the true state of their souls. Thousands of other matters of less importance preoccupy their time and energies, and if they pray at all, it is to offer fleeting requests a few times a month. As a rule, their minds are fixed on the worldly preoccupations to which they are attached.

Once in a while they are reminded of the words of our Lord: "Where your treasure is, there your heart will be also" (Matthew 6:21). Then, for a moment at least, they put aside their worldly pursuits because they have been startled into seeing that they are not growing spiritually.

And so these people run back and stand just within the gateway of their souls, because it is important to them only to know they are safe. At least they enter the first rooms of the castle. But these are the lowest rooms of the soul and, like the lowest rooms of an earthly castle, there are so many "reptiles" and crawling things here that they cannot see the beauty of the castle's deep interior. They experience nothing of inner tranquility and suppose that such heavenly-peace-on-earth does not exist.

These people think they have done enough just by entering in at the right gate. In their arrogance—though they do not see it as arrogance—they think God is just wonderfully pleased that they have come to Him at all.

THE INTERIOR CASTLE

My Heavenly Father, sometimes every voice within me shouts a warning—that I must be careful of becoming too "over-zealous" or "fanatical."

Today, Father, show me the earthly possessions that have trapped me . . . the positions of worldly honor or power that keep me from serving you . . . the people whose approval I want more than I want yours.

24
Our Confidence

Your attitude should be the same as that of Christ Jesus: Who, being in very nature God, did not consider equality with God something to be grasped, but made himself nothing, taking the very nature of a servant. . . .

Philippians 2:5–7

His Majesty is so good and so giving—and yet we have such stingy hearts toward Him.

We think we will lose the whole world if we work to subdue the appetites of the body even a little for the sake of growing in spirit. Then we offer this argument: It helps me to feel secure when I know my needs are taken care of—otherwise I'm too upset to pray with any measure of peace.

How painful to think that our confidence in God is so weak and our love of self so strong that the least anxiety about our needs should disturb our prayer life—when prayer is the very means to our peace! Yet it is so. Small matters shake our peace. . . . And we think ourselves spiritual!

Enter, my friends—enter into the castle of our King. Get beyond those miserable good works of yours, which you think you are required to do to prove you are a Christian. Let this be enough for you: that you are a lowly subject of the Most High King. Let this be your upward goal and nothing more.

Consider the many men and women of God who know how to enter into the chamber of the King. You will see by their lives what a difference there is between them and us. True, we would like to be like them, but for most that is a fleshly desire—for we would like to have the same honor given to them, but we do not want to walk the low path they have walked on their way to spiritual heights. . . .

Oh, humility—*humility!*

THE INTERIOR CASTLE

My Generous Father, sometimes I secretly hope for thanks or appreciation for doing a kindness for someone.

Root out of me any need to be appreciated that would keep me from knowing your praise . . . receiving my thanks . . . in serving you alone.

You . . . your presence with me . . . this is my best reward.

Secret Pride

The man and his wife heard the sound of the Lord God . . . and they hid. . . . But the Lord God called to the man, "Where are you?"
He answered, "I heard you in the garden, and I was afraid, because I was naked. . . ."

Genesis 3:8–10

Seek the Lord while he may be found; call on him while he is near . . . turn to the Lord, and he will have mercy on [you], and to our God, for he will freely pardon.

Isaiah 55:6–7

My purpose in my previous piece of writing about humility was to show you how to incline the attitude of your heart.

By that I mean you are to make yourself fully subject to God in all that He sends into your life and all that He allows to be removed from you— whether of honor, possessions, friends, or health.

In this way, you can help yourself to some degree in these beginning matters of devotion to God. . . .

But beware, lest you fall into pride on this point. For devotion is not earned or achieved by our efforts. It comes by grace, as God allows it, or it does not really come at all. . . .

Yes, in our present state we can resolve to obey God and do the good works He calls us to do. And we can meditate on the sacrificial suffering of our Lord, who died for our sakes. . . . We can also meditate on His sacred humanity, which will cause us to act compassionately toward others, and in doing so we place ourselves in the presence of Christ (Matthew 25:40).

Yet I hardly know how to warn you about a serious temptation that comes upon you when you are on this spiritual path. It happens like this, best as I can describe it for you: First, you feel dry in spirit. Then you become aware of your spiritual dryness. And when it goes on for some time, you can become overly concerned about yourself.

This is the fine point you must not miss if you would continue to grow in spirit: The moment you focus on your *self* again, you place yourself in the center of your attentions and not the Lord!

I am trying to warn you. Do not dwell upon your inner failings. . . . Instead, merely accept the fact that you are a easily failing creature, given to times of spiritual dryness. Do not become restless and anxious about yourself, saying, "Look how terrible and feeble I am—too terrible for God to heal or to change me." If you do, you are playing into the devil's hand, for this spiritual pride is exactly what he wants.

. . . Just do this: Bring your soul to the Great Physician—exactly as you are, even and *especially* in your worst moment. Simply agree with Him that you are soul-sick indeed. For it is in such moments that you will most readily sense His healing presence, and only then that He can begin to heal your worst spiritual diseases. . . .

THE LIFE . . . and THE INTERIOR CASTLE

My Father—Great Physician, you know that I hate to fail, especially when others see me fail.

Forgive me for thinking I am "better than that," and for trying to conceal sins and failings from you . . . as if I could.

Give me a heart of thankfulness for the one whose words or actions break through my nice smooth "veneer," exposing the places in my heart where your kingdom has yet to come.

26
New Covenant
. . . of Love

From everlasting to everlasting the Lord's love is with those who fear him. . . .

Psalm 103:17

[Even] if we are faithless, he will remain faithful. . . .

2 Timothy 2:13

This is the message you heard from the beginning: . . . Love one another.

1 John 3:11

When we hope to gain affection from others, we always seek it because of some interest, benefit or pleasure we hope to receive from them. . . .

However "pure" our affection for another may

seem in our own eyes, it is natural that we should want them to feel affection for us. Too often, though, we begin to analyze the affection they show us. Do they feel the same toward us as we feel toward them? Would they do as much for us? Soon we determine that, compared with the way we feel for them, compared with what we would do for them, their love for us has little substance. "It is like a piece of chaff in the wind, insignificant and easily blown away."

I want you to consider this, though: No matter how dearly we have been loved by any human being—what is there in human love that is not "chaff"? And what is it that remains?

The one who truly loves in spirit . . . cares nothing whether he receives the affection of another or not. When I say this, you may think it odd and unnatural. You may think that such a person will be cold and compassionless toward people while they are occupied with loving God.

Nothing is further from the truth. A man or woman who learns to love in a detached manner, for the sake of God's love, will love others a great deal. They will love with greater compassion and greater intensity. Their only concern will be to see the person they love grow in the Lord, no matter what it takes.

To love others for *their* spiritual profit and not for our own comfort or benefit—that is what love really is. People who love in this way are always more happy to give than to receive, even in their relationship with the Creator himself!

So many other things have been described as affection, when they are really only base and self-seeking. What I have described to you is true *holy* affection. It is the only thing that deserves to be called by its high and holy name: Love.

THE WAY OF PERFECTION

My Perfect Father, sometimes love would require me to keep silent and bear with another in long-suffering patience. Sometimes I'm afraid to speak because I don't want to look unkind.

Teach me—for your kingdom's sake, and not for mine—how to love perfectly the one who is seeking or struggling.

27
Wealth and Honor

[Jesus] began to teach them, saying, "Blessed are the poor in spirit, for theirs is the kingdom of heaven."

Matthew 5:2–3

As believers in our glorious Lord Jesus Christ, don't show favoritism. . . . Has not God chosen those who are poor in the eyes of the world to be rich in faith and to inherit the kingdom he promised those who love him?

James 2:1, 5

You must believe me when I tell you . . . what blessings are to be found in learning to be detached from all your material possessions. . . .

Although I used to say that my possessions had no hold over me, it was not true at all. I was not "poor in spirit" in the least. In fact, if my heart attached itself to some object of desire, I had no restraint whatever, and had to possess it or my heart would give me no rest.

123

That is why I now say it is so good to practice spiritual poverty. By that I mean I have learned to see, with the eyes of my heart, that no possession can give the eternal joy my soul hungers for. More than that, because earthly possessions give a measure of short-lived satisfaction, they can actually be a snare that keeps you from ever seeking the eternal joy that is not dependent upon what you own.

The practice of spiritual poverty leads you into a wonderful kingdom. Here, paradoxically, you find yourself free to enjoy all the good things of the world. For the man or woman who has no cares about worldly goods is, in spirit, lord over all of them, for possessions do not rule and direct their lives.

What do kings and other earthly rulers matter to me if I have no desire to impress them so they will give me their money—and no desire to please them at all, for that matter, if in doing so I displease God? And what do the honors they bestow on other men mean to me?

No, I tell you that I have seen with the eyes of my heart that the man or woman who does not depend at all on this world's goods has the highest honor in God's sight!

For honor and money always go together. The one who wants to be honored by other men is nearly always trapped into the love of money, because worldly people love money so much that they automatically give great honor to the one who has much money, no matter how little deserving of honor or respect he may be. . . .

If you embrace this virtue—desiring to be poor in heart because you want to learn to love and rely on God, and Him alone—then you are free indeed. For your soul will not be bound to any man, and you will not live to please anyone, except God.

The man or woman who has no need of anyone is free to be the friend of everyone.

THE WAY OF PERFECTION

My Father—Provider, Owner of all, set me free from judging the worth of others based on what they own or what they have accomplished.

And begin to set me free from any possession I have . . . or secretly long for . . . that is keeping my heart from being your pure possession.

28
Blame

Jesus said . . . "Blessed are you when people insult you, persecute you and falsely say all kinds of evil against you because of me. Rejoice and be glad, because great is your reward in heaven. . . ."

Matthew 5:11–12

These twelve Jesus sent out with the following instructions: . . . "A student is not above his teacher, nor a servant his master. . . . If the head of the house has been [wrongly accused, and insulted], how much more the members of his household!"

Matthew 10:5, 24–25

What strange thing is this, my Lord?—that there is anything to gain by winning the approval and favor of other men and women. After all, they are only created beings, as we are.

It does not matter one whit if everyone speaks highly of me. It matters only that I live without blame in your sight, my Lord!

I beg you to see this, my friends: We will never begin to understand the truth, nor will we begin to walk in the way of spiritual perfection unless we fix our minds and our souls on the difference between eternal realities and earthly realities.

The person who blames you unjustly will be confused if he sees you accept the condemnation with the peace that comes from resting completely in God. And you can only rest in Him if, with spiritual eyes, you behold Him always before you—your Lord, who, alone, is the wise and loving judge of all. If you behold your invisible, loving Lord and stand in peace, while your accuser falls back in confusion—isn't that in itself a reward for learning patience?

Such an experience lifts the soul more than ten sermons on "why a Christian should be patient." It is more important that we all become "preachers" by our godly actions. . . .

Or is it that you think wrongly about our Lord? Do you think that if you do not stand up for yourself, no one else will defend you? Consider how the Lord took Mary Magdalene's part when she came into the Pharisee's house and threw herself at Jesus' feet, sinful woman that she was, and the Pharisee wanted to throw her out. . . .

Have no fear, the Lord will not let you suffer the condemnation as long as He allowed himself to bear the wrongful blame of men. It was not until He was nailed and left to die on the cross that He allowed a condemned thief to defend Him. His Majesty will put it into someone's mind to defend you. And if He does not, it is because He knows there is no need to defend.

But I do not want you always to be looking for a defense at all! Rather I say: Be happy when you are blamed and accused wrongly, for then you have the chance to see all the bitter, hostile, or self-pitying responses that your sinful soul wants to spew out—as if these puny things could in any way defend you! Watch and see if any of these poisons come out of you when your spirit is pricked by an accusation. Only then can you see yourself as you are, and confess the sin that is within you, and forsake yourself again into the Lord's care.

Hard though it may seem to you now, this is the way that you begin to gain freedom. And soon you will not care if others speak poorly of you, or if they speak well. In either case, it will seem as if they are discussing someone else in your hearing. . . .

No doubt this seems impossible to those among us who are very sensitive. Indeed, to those dear souls, putting to death their sweet, delicate flesh seems impossible. True, it will be more difficult for them—at first.

But I know this for a fact: The Lord is our Helper. And gradually, all who seek to walk in His Spirit can allow the blame of others to help set them free from their need for the approval of men. By His help, we can renounce our dependence upon men, and become detached from our *self*, which demands to be seen in the best light.

My Wise Father—and My only *Judge, you alone walk the pathways of my inmost heart. And you know where the roots of my soul try to draw strength and a secure hold from the good opinions of others.*

I give you permission to weed out my insistent need for others to think highly of me . . . when men did not think highly of you.

29
Sons Who Serve

Jesus called [his disciples, who were arguing,]
together and said, "You know that the rulers of the
Gentiles lord it over them, and their high officials
exercise authority over them. Not so with you.
Instead, whoever wants to become great among you
must be your servant, and whoever wants to be first
must be your slave—just as the Son of Man did not
come to be served, but to serve,
and to give his life. . . ."

Matthew 20:25–28

[Jesus taught them, saying,] "If someone strikes you
on the right cheek, turn to him the other also. . . .
I tell you: Love your enemies
and pray for those who persecute you,
that you may be sons
of your Father in heaven."

Matthew 5:39, 44–45

We say that we want to share in the

kingdom of our Lord. And we certainly want to enjoy the blessings and the benefits the spiritual life seems to offer.

Yet we are not willing in the least to accept any of the fiery trials by which our souls would be purified. In short, we say we want to live in our Lord's kingdom—but we do not want to suffer the dishonoring of the flesh that He suffered.

This is ridiculous. May God keep us from such spiritual blindness, such unhappy foolishness.

Will you accept this word from our Lord: The one who is counted least among you is the greatest.

Count yourself most fortunate—happy indeed!—if people overlook you, take no notice of you, or treat you with little respect. For then you have the opportunity to seek only the respect of God himself. If you make this a spiritual principle that guides your life, you will have no lack of honor in this life (at least in the eyes of truly spiritual people), and you will be honored when you finally step from this life into the next. Believe me when I tell you this!

. . . Be on your guard, then. For someone is bound to offend you, and then there is the chance for temptation upon temptation to trap you.

First, you may be hurt by the offense itself. And then you may be more deeply offended because this person was so careless and so disrespectful. Then you are no longer hurt by their misdeed or their ill-spoken word—you are deeply wounded that they did not respect you merely as a person. This I call *being punctilious about your honor*.

Rather that you should die a thousand deaths than fall into a spiritual pit so deep. For then only the body would die, whereas losing your soul for the sake of a worldly honor is a terrible loss indeed.

THE WAY OF PERFECTION

My Father, is there something in me that is offended over and over again?

Show me where my honor and ego still reign.

Thank you, Father, that you love me and uphold me while you do your deepest, most painful work.

30
Our "Boast"

If I must boast, I will boast of the things that show my weakness. . . . I pleaded with the Lord to take [my thorn in the flesh, a messenger of Satan] away from me. But he said to me, "My grace is sufficient for you, for my power is made perfect in weakness." Therefore I will boast all the more gladly about my weaknesses, so that Christ's power may rest on me.

2 Corinthians 11:30; 12:8–9

Sometimes we fall into a complaining mood and think we need to complain about every ache and pain, every sad feeling that comes over us. This is a great mistake, and a snare used by the evil one. . . .

Our troubles—in body and in soul—come and go, like everything else that is temporal. Unless you first get rid of the bad habit of complaining about them—indeed of *complaining at all*—you will never overcome the flesh, and it will always rule over you.

I do not mean that you should stop talking

over your troubles with God. That would be a mistake, for He tells us to cast all of our cares and heavy burdens upon Him (Psalm 55:22; Matthew 11:28).

Yet when we make a habit of complaining, it is because we are allowing ourselves to relax in our inward spiritual walk that sifts and transforms the heart. How sad, because following the spiritual path—that is, allowing God to sift and purify our hearts by every means—would *free* us in spirit from earthly complaints!

Make no mistake: The more you indulge your flesh, the more it will tell you, "I cannot live without this and that small luxury—I *need* it, so God cannot mean that it should be taken from me. That's fanaticism." It is amazing how much our body loves to be indulged. The flesh will use any pretense at all to whine and insist that it is not strong, or that being denied any little thing is just too much to bear—never mind that God may have sent the exact circumstances to remove such and such a fleshly weight from us!

So, through our own complaining and insistence upon our "needs," we prevent our own souls from making progress toward freedom in Christ.

Learn to put up with pain, hardship and loss—even a little bit—for the sake of knowing God's love for you in deeper measure. Do so without telling everyone you know the details of all your aches and pains. . . . Can't you learn to hold this as a secret between God and you? Or do you not believe that His presence with you, bearing you up and strengthening you in hardship, is enough for you?

This is a hard saying, I know, but it is true nonetheless: God allows sickness and suffering in our lives in order to sift out our soul's sinful dependence upon physical strength, or our need for the sympathies of others.

You would think that more Christians would accept a deeper spiritual view in this matter, since all of our complaining about hardships does nothing whatever to relieve them—and in fact, it makes our hardships much harder to bear, since it keeps them always before us. . . .

THE WAY OF PERFECTION

My Comforting Father, I have seen how weak I am in spirit . . . and how much I need to trust you to grow me in your strength.

Teach me, daily, to depend only on you, Lord. Be the burning light that guides me . . . close at my side . . . through the dark and difficult valleys of my life.

31
Standard Bearers

In that day the Root of Jesse will stand as a banner for the peoples. . . .

Isaiah 11:10

Jesus said, . . . "Now the prince of this world will be driven out. But I, when I am lifted up from the earth, will draw all men to myself."

John 12:30–32

If you choose to walk the inner path with God—that is, if you would be pure in heart, growing in the perfect likeness of our Lord—then you cannot involve yourself in warfare on lesser matters.

Some would argue that when you choose to grow in the inner life, you are not involved in warfare of spirit at all—but in fact, you are exposed to great dangers and, inwardly, you will suffer and struggle more than any other soldier in this spiritual war in which we are all engaged.

Why? Because the one who would imitate our Lord in the perfect humility I have been telling you about is the *standard bearer*, going before the army of God. Because his rank is to carry the standard, he cannot "bear arms," as others can, to defend himself at all. His place in the ranks is to lift the standard high and never to let it fall from his hands, even if it means that he is cut to pieces by the enemy.

If you would be one of God's standard bearers, you must lift up *humility* for all to see. And to do so, you must completely lower your self, accepting every blow and insult without striking back or lifting a finger to defend. The calling and duty of a standard bearer is to suffer in the same manner that Christ did. It is to lift high the cross, and never let it fall, no matter what difficulty or loss you face. . . .

It is for the honor and the sake of Christ himself that you are called to such honorable duty. If you are one who is given this type of spiritual vision—if you can see and understand this with the eyes of your soul—you will know how vital is your role. For you will see that if you let the standard fall, the battle is lost.

Great spiritual harm is done to those who are new in the faith when those they look up to as captains and friends of God refuse to walk in the Spirit and, instead, take up the struggle in the flesh, which betrays their spiritual calling.

THE WAY OF PERFECTION

My Father—Lord and Commander, I
thank you that you train me for the spiritual fight . . .
and that you never leave me when the battle gets thick.
Set the eyes of my heart on Jesus, who is the
Captain of my faith . . . and my standard of humility.

32
Search Me Within

Surely you desire truth in the inner parts; you teach
me wisdom in the inmost place. Cleanse me . . . and I
will be clean. . . .

Psalm 51:6-7

Search me, O God, and know my heart; test me and
know my anxious thoughts. See if there is any
offensive way in me, and lead me in the way
everlasting.

Psalm 139:23–24

. . . do [everything] with gentleness and respect,
keeping a clear conscience. . . .

1 Peter 3:15, 16

If we keep a pure conscience before God, we
will suffer no harm—or, at least, the blows we
experience in our earthly lives will only serve to
drive us deeper into dependence and
commitment to God.

For that is the whole point of pain and tribulations: to help us sift through our innermost thoughts toward God, and to see if we carry any secret anger or judgment or resistance or sense of offense toward Him. I hope that you will never stop allowing God to examine your soul, exposing to your conscience the points at which you hold wicked, self-exalting thoughts against God.

When we love God so much that we side with Him against ourselves—when we fear separating ourselves from Him so much as a hairsbreadth in opinion and will, it is *then* that we keep ourselves in good standing with our King. For then we walk in true spiritual agreement with Him.

Oh, what a tremendous thing it is to live in the light with the Lord—that is, to live without any offense or disagreement between us. For then the messengers and slaves of hell have no power over us, no matter what they do and say. And think of this, too: In the end, we will all bow our knees to His almighty lordship—either by force, or by wholehearted choice.

If we serve God with a clean conscience—holding nothing between us, seeking always and only to please Him—the minions of hell will be kept at bay. Though they may for a moment cause us to be unsettled, they will have no power whatever to bring lasting harm. And make no mistake, they *will* lead us into temptations and set traps for us all along the way!

Have this understanding then—that God loves you and, to keep you walking in the light with Him, He will sift you. For then you will not neglect your soul's condition, but you will find that you are developing a fixed determination to please the Lord. You will find that you would rather suffer and lose a thousand lives—you would rather be persecuted by the entire world than to offend God in any way great or small. . . .

From any sin, great or small, committed while knowing that we are going against God's will— may God deliver us. How can we keep sinning against so great a Sovereign, especially when we know we can walk in His light and His presence—especially when we know He is watching us?

THE WAY OF PERFECTION

My Father—Light all-seeing and all-consuming, I have felt you sifting my heart, and I've been afraid to look at the things your sifting has uncovered.

But I thank you that you search me only to unburden me . . . heal me . . . set me more free in you.

I love you, Father, for the light you shed on my inner ways.

33
The Sign

Jesus said, . . . "All men will know that you are my disciples if you love one another."

———

John 13:31-35

*L*ove is a great fire, and it will do nothing but give out a very bright light that will attract others to God.

If any Christian does not have love in his life, he should stop and consider this deficiency very carefully. Do not think you can go on in your spiritual growth. No, if we are not growing in love, we should be filled with dread, for something is very wrong.

If you find that you are without love toward anyone, this is what you must do—for you will not go on with the Lord unless you resolve this matter in your spirit:

Go to God in honest prayer.

Open yourself to Him in the spirit of humility—which means asking Him to sift your heart and show you where wicked self-exaltation is causing you to lift yourself up and think you are better than your brother.

Beg the Lord to keep you from any temptation that causes you to keep falling into the sin of pride. It is pride that keeps us blind to our own sins, but so loveless that we are always aware of the smallest sins of others. And so we ask God to correct and judge them, but to spare us! (Matthew 7:1–5).

Unless you open your soul to God in this way—that is, *completely*—you will never bear the sign of the one who is a true believer in Jesus Christ. That sign is *love*. . . .

If you want to grow in your love for God, then your attitude of heart must change. You must be so loathe to offend Him that you stop acting as if you are superior to others. Then, I tell you, your inner life will become one of peace and tranquility.

THE WAY OF PERFECTION

My Father, just as your Son bore the signs of love in His own flesh . . . let me willingly bear the signs of love in my life.

Open my eyes, today, to your great sacrifice of love . . . for my sake.

34
Law of the Kingdom

For to us a child is born, to us a son is given, and the government will be on his shoulders.

Isaiah 9:6

Jesus said, "As the Father has loved me, so have I loved you. Now remain in my love. If you obey my commands, you will remain in my love, just as I have obeyed my Father's commands and remain in his love. . . . My command is this: Love each other as I have loved you."

John 15:9–10, 12

If you want to make great advances in prayer . . . if you want to walk the "high road" in spirit and reach the chambers of the King, then you must remember this:

The truest, deepest prayer—that is, spiritual communion with God—does not consist in how much we know of doctrines or of spiritual truth. True prayer consists in how much we are set free to love.

With that understanding, then, I tell you: *Do with your life whatever will set you free to give the most love.*

I wonder if most of us even know what spiritual love is. It does not mean that we experience greater emotional delights. It means that, because we see God as He is, we experience a stronger resolve to please Him—in fact, an unquenchable desire to please Him no matter what. It means that we grow in such a way that, more and more, we want to please Him in everything, offend Him in nothing.

If we love Him, we will find ourselves begging Him to do whatever is necessary to lift up the honor and glory of His Son. In this way—by our prayers and by the loving witness of our lives— the borders of His Church are spread far and wide.

These are the signs that the love of God is governing in our lives.

THE INTERIOR CASTLE

My Father—Father of all, I know you have created me with a perfect plan in mind.

Today, I will eagerly look for chances to bring your light and love . . . to spread your kingdom in the Spirit . . . as you open the way for me to love others.

35
Water of Life

*Hear the word of the Lord. . . . The Lord will
ransom . . . and redeem. . . . [You] will be like a
well-watered garden, and [you] will sorrow no more.*

Jeremiah 31:10-12

*You, [my bride] . . . are a garden fountain, a well of
flowing water. . . ."*

Song of Songs 4:12, 15

*Jesus answered, . . . "Whoever drinks the water I
give him will never thirst. Indeed, the water I give
him will become in him a spring of water welling up
to eternal life."*

John 4:13-14

Learning to draw water up from the spiritual
well is a hard labor, indeed—at least in the
beginning.

It is difficult, in the first place, to keep all of

your senses recollected and focused upon total humility before God. What a tremendous difficulty this is, because our senses are so much in the habit of flitting about from one worldly distraction to another. And so you must learn to set aside what you see and hear in order to see and hear what God would pour out upon you from His invisible kingdom.

You must keep warring in spirit to fix your inmost thoughts on the life of Christ. When you do this, you go beyond the limits of your human understanding. And this is a very good thing, because our understanding is of the flesh, and it cannot comprehend—much less accept—the way in which our Lord so totally set aside His own manly will in order to live in complete obedience to the Father.

When we begin to renew our minds in this way—that is, building the habit of constantly, deeply meditating upon the Lord Jesus—we draw water up out of the deep wells of salvation (Isaiah 12:3).

So, this is our part in the work: to wrestle with our wandering senses and our flitting thoughts. And God's part is to enliven our meditations by the power of His Spirit, so that it becomes for us living water—and this part, of course, does not depend upon us at all; it depends upon God.

In this way, the tender "flowers" of new

spiritual growth are "watered."

THE LIFE OF THERESA OF JESUS

*M*ajestic Father—*Spring of Living Water, you give me refreshment for my soul. Thank you for Jesus, who is my healing and my forgiveness.*

Today, let me offer the refreshing words of healing and forgiveness to another.

36
The River

*T*he man [in white linen] brought me back to the
entrance to the temple, and I saw water coming out
from under the threshold of the temple . . . the water
was flowing . . . and [he] led me through water that
was ankle deep . . . knee deep . . . up to the waist
. . . deep enough to swim in—a river that no one
could cross. He asked me, "Son of man, do you see
this?"

Ezekiel 47:1–6

I did not see a temple in the city [that came down
from heaven—the city of God!] because the Lord God
Almighty and the Lamb are its temple . . . the angel
showed me the river of the water of life, as clear as
crystal, flowing from the throne of God and of the
Lamb.

Revelation 21:22; 22:1

*H*alfway through the Feast [of Passover] did Jesus go
up to the temple courts and begin to teach. . . . On
the last and greatest day of the Feast, Jesus stood and

said in a loud voice, "If anyone is thirsty, let him come to me and drink. Whoever believes in me, as the Scripture has said, streams of living water will flow from within him."

—————

John 7:14, 37–38

You may wonder how anyone can be confident whether a spiritual experience is true.

First, you must realize that the devil is not capable of touching our souls with a pain that is so delightful—and a true spiritual experience is both an agony and a joy. The devil can give us pain—in the form of guilt or terror—or he can give us delights that arouse the flesh. And for some, these will be mistaken for "spiritual experiences." I assure you, it is beyond the devil's power to unite both of these powerful forces into anything good.

Only God is capable of awakening our souls with a joy so sweet that it is, at the same time, a longing for Him that is also painful and intense. When this happens, then every part of our mortal flesh falls quiet and still, and our soul is set afloat in a beautiful self-forgetfulness that is like a stream—no, a deep river—of joy.

The devil's strength can only affect us outwardly, with trials of the flesh and outward opposition through others who are in his grasp. Or else he goads us with inward condemnation and turbulence and restlessness. The trials he sends, like arrows, are not peaceful or sweet in the least.

. . . The spiritual experiences I am talking about will always cause you to choose to lay aside all rights and honors, and to follow God more faithfully, even if it means suffering and persecution. In short, they help you to put to death the deeds of the flesh and to open the soul to more of the life of God. How could this be from the devil?

Yes, when God moves upon the soul it will be most evident. For the soul will receive new determination to give up more worldly pleasures and to stop seeking its honor and power from worldly pursuits. Instead, it will be more at peace to rest in God's hand no matter what is sent— even pain or affliction.

Do you call this "mere fancy"? It is not. And the devil can never counterfeit such a state of total rest, which comes only from the Spirit of God.

THE INTERIOR CASTLE

My Father—my deep River of Peace, how can I thank you—that Jesus has given me the white robes of salvation, purchased with His holy and human blood!—and that you pour out your Holy Spirit as a River of Life today!

Keep my soul, Father, as I grow deeper in you, and

serve you, and tell others what I know of you. Give me a purer resolve, with each new morning, to live and move and have my being . . . only for your good pleasure.

37
Light That Leads, Truth That Frees

When can I go and meet with God? . . . Deep calls to deep. . . . Send forth your light and your truth . . . let them bring me to your holy mountain, to the place where you dwell.

Psalm 42:2, 7; 43:3

*O*ur Lord has many ways of leading the soul until it is fully awake—and one of these ways is by speaking to us.

It may seem that the one to whom the Lord speaks in this way is especially favored above all the rest of us. But in fact, there is more danger in these holy "words" from God. So I will take some time to give you guidance on this matter. . . .

Some of these "words" will seem to come from outside yourself. Others seem to come from somewhere deep within your own soul. At other times, it seems as if a voice is calling from somewhere high above—and sometimes it seems so loud and real that it seems as if we have actually heard audible words, like those spoken by men of flesh and blood. . . .

There are many souls who hear the voice of God in these various ways. . . . I warn you: If such a thing happens to you, do not think that you are more highly favored by God than others. Remember that our Lord spoke frequently even with those white-washed sepulchers, the Pharisees!

Any good that can come out of such a spiritual experience will depend on whether or not we take advantage of the words our Lord speaks to us.

Therefore, pay no attention to any spiritual message that does not conform in the strictest sense with the Holy Scriptures. If it contradicts the principles of Scripture in the least point, treat it as if it were a message from Satan. . . .

But if the words do indeed come from God, then it makes no difference where we think they come from—whether from "above" or "within," whether audible or not. The most important evidence that a message comes from God—which is all that matters—is this: The words will come bearing an authority that you will sense at once, and they will also have a transforming power. . . .

For instance, a soul may be overwhelmed with anxiety, torn with restlessness, like a storm-driven sea. Or it may feel deathly dryness, like a desert. Or confused, and lacking in all spiritual understanding or direction. All of the scholars in the world may converge upon this soul, and heap upon it reasons why it should not feel grief and abandonment. And if they are not speaking with the voice of the Spirit to this afflicted soul, their words will all be as *nothing*. . . .

But if one of them brings the living Word—*"It is I; do not be afraid"*—the soul will be freed in an instant from every anxiety, though not a detail of its outward circumstances has been changed.

If, as a result, true joy comes to reign in the life of this believer—joy that springs from the unshakable conviction that nothing can separate them from God himself—how can this be anything other than a true spiritual experience? (Romans 8:38-39).

THE INTERIOR CASTLE

My Father—Word of Truth, I used to seek your word as a way to comfort myself in my darkness. No longer will I be afraid when your living Word begins to burn me with holy fire and with strong conviction.

But guard my mouth so that I don't speak presumptuously . . . wrongly assuming that I know the words you would speak to someone else.

38

By Water . . . By Fire

Jesus answered, "I tell you the truth, no one can enter the kingdom of God unless he is born of water and the Spirit. Flesh gives birth to flesh, but the Spirit gives birth to spirit."

———

John 3:5–6

[Jesus] gave them this command: ". . . Wait for the gift my Father promised, which you have heard me speak about. . . . You will receive power when the Holy Spirit comes on you; and you will be my witnesses . . ."

———

Acts 1:4, 8

Suddenly a sound like the blowing of a violent wind came from heaven. . . . They saw what seemed to be tongues of fire that separated and came to rest on each of them.

———

Acts 2:2–3

What a marvelous thing—when the fire of God burns fierce and strong within us, nothing on earth can quench it.

And what a delightful irony that, in spiritual terms, the water of the Spirit only makes the fire of our faith grow brighter and hotter. . . .

If God grants you to drink living water from the deep wells of salvation, your faith will grow powerful indeed. Once you taste this water, you will be given such a strong love for God that you will be completely released from a false love for earthly things. You will be able to rise above every snare and temptation—a master over all the elements, and of the whole world. . . .

The one on whom the fire of God comes to rest is master of all things, subject to nothing. You will not be surprised, then, when I urge you with all my heart: Strive in the Spirit to have this kind of fiery faith, for it is the source of wonderful freedom.

Is it not a great joke that an ordinary woman like myself should attain such mastery over the whole earth? Why do we wonder, then, that the saints who went before us commanded even the elements, with the powerful help of God, and they obeyed? Since they were helped by God to do miracles, and since they were laying their lives before God in complete obedience, they could almost have claimed this power as a right—but they knew better. . . .

There are other things we mistake for this

unquenchable fire I am speaking of—emotions, gratitude for some blessing, the warmth of Christian fellowship or kindness. But this type of "love for God" will almost invariably be quenched when the blessing ceases.

But the fire that lights upon our souls from heaven is this: *a love for the high honor of God himself.*

This fire, I tell you, can never be quenched.

THE WAY OF PERFECTION

Father of Holy Fire, in all things that I do today, however simple or great, let me act out of reverence for you . . . out of love and respect for others, whom you call me to serve . . .

Let my greatest honor be this—that others may hear me speak, or watch my actions . . . and think more highly of you.

39
The King in "Check"

*S*ubmit yourselves, then, to God. Resist the devil,
and he will flee from you. Come near to God and he
will come near to you. Wash your hands . . . purify
your hearts. . . . Humble yourselves before the
Lord, and he will lift you up.

James 4:7–10, emphasis added

*Y*ou asked me to tell you about the steps that
will lead into a deeper inner life. . . . I know no
others than all the ones I have taken time to tell
you about. . . .

I will tell you one thing more, though—
knowing that some will disapprove of me for
using the example of a chess game to illustrate
something about our relationship with God. . . .

Yet I think this is legitimate, because I want to
tell you how you may give checkmate to the
Divine King. If you make the "moves" I suggest,
He will not be able to move out of your "check"—

and He will be pleased to have been "captured" in this way!

As you may know, it is the queen who gives the king the most trouble in this game. An experienced player knows that all the other pieces only support her, and they set up the board in preparation for her to make her moves and win the whole match.

In our "match" with the King, there is nothing that can "beat" Him as well as humility—that is, the attitude of heart that places ourselves in God's hands, fully trusting Him.

Humility is the queen of the godly virtues.

Humility brought our King down from heaven, into the womb of the virgin. When we act in humility, we act in His name and in the very thing that was His greatest power—and so we draw Him down from heaven to live in us and to be "born again" into this world through our lives. And He will be our helper, too (John 14:16), giving more spiritual power to him who humbly relinquishes his life for the sake of God, and taking away from him who merely seeks his own position and honor (Matthew 25:28).

Keep in mind that you cannot rest in God in the kind of complete humility I am talking about unless you know that God is love. And you should never deceive yourself into thinking you are living in godly humility unless His love flows out of you toward others.

Here is a secret: God's love and His humility

can never exist in you unless you grow in this state of detachment from everything that is of this world. As long as any created thing has power over you, you cannot "rule" over it in the love and humility of our King.

THE WAY OF PERFECTION

My Humble Father, I have seen you in the beauty of your holiness . . . and you have captivated my soul with longing for you.

In my deep motives . . . my thoughts . . . my words . . . my actions . . . let me live more and more in your presence . . . in the embrace of simple obedience to you.

40
Bound for His Kingdom

Jesus declared, . . . "He who believes in me will never
be thirsty. . . . For my Father's will is that everyone
who looks to the Son and believes in him shall have
eternal life, and I will raise him up. . . ."

John 6:35, 40

And [the angel] carried me away in the Spirit to a
mountain great and high, and showed me the Holy
City, Jerusalem, coming down out of heaven from
God. . . . The Spirit and the bride say, "Come!" . . .
Whoever is thirsty, let him come; and whoever wishes,
let him take the free gift of the water of life."

Revelation 21:10; 22:17

We, as His Majesty's servants, will
sometimes forget our life's true purpose. Then He
will beckon us again with His call from above,
and we will feel in our hearts a deep and tender

171

longing for the joy of God's presence. We will long to leave this land of shadowy exile. . . .

But since we want to do His will, we turn from our own weak longings and desire only to fulfill His will here on earth every day as long as we live. And it is no small thing to reflect on the fact that He is with us—He himself in His beautiful majestic presence.

We need only to know this: *He will never leave us!*

Resting in this knowledge, your soul will remain well-fed, and completely satisfied. . . .

The one who has this holy knowledge is set free and rises in spirit. No longer does he long for anything on lowly earth to console him—nor does he have need for earthly answers and comforts, because he knows Christ our Lord is with him always. Or, to say it rightly: *His Majesty now lives within us.*

. . . Therefore, we are let loose to fly above all things. Whether we are alone, or we are in the midst of painstaking labor for the well-being of some other soul, we are not bound or subject to any earthly thing. In this spiritual state no dryness of spirit need overcome you, and no distress can weigh you down.

Always remember that His Majesty is with you. And pray every day that your spirit be kept tender and obedient in His sweet service.

May your life become one of glad and unending praise to the Lord as you journey

through this world, and in the world that is to
come!

*My Father, how majestic is your name!
How great is your rule over every part of my life!*

*Today, and in all my days to come, keep me close to
you. Shape me more in your image. Work through me,
as your obedient child.*

*Make me ready and full of praises . . . as I walk in
this world . . . destined to stand, at last, before your
shining throne!*

DAVID HAZARD developed the REKINDLING THE INNER FIRE devotional series to encourage others to keep the "heart" of their faith alive and afire with love for God. He also feels a special need to help Christians of today to "meet" men and women of the past whose experience of God belongs to the whole Church, for all the ages.

Hazard is an award-winning writer, the author of books for both adults and children, with international bestsellers among his many titles. He lives in northern Virginia with his wife, MaryLynne, and three children: Aaron, Joel, and Sarah Beth.